FROM THERE TO ETERNITY
ALZHEIMER'S AND BEYOND

D1601893

From There to Eternity

Alzheimer's and Beyond

F. Harlan Flint

SUNSTONE PRESS
SANTA FE

Book and Cover Concept
by
Nicole Rassmuson

Artisan Minds
Brand and Communication Design
Santa Fe, New Mexico

Sunstone books may be purchased for educational, business, or sales promotional use.
For information please write: Special Markets Department, Sunstone Press,
P.O. Box 2321, Santa Fe, New Mexico 87504-2321.
Printed on acid-free paper

Library of Congress Cataloging-in-Publication Data

Names: Flint, F. Harlan, 1930- author.
Title: From there to eternity : Alzheimer's and beyond / F. Harlan Flint.
Description: Santa Fe : Sunstone Press, [2021] | Summary: "The death
  sentence of Alzheimer's redeemed by old friends and new"-- Provided by
  publisher.
Identifiers: LCCN 2020057873 | ISBN 9781632933171 (paperback) | ISBN
  9781611396195 (epub)
Subjects: LCSH: Flint, Christine Mason. | Alzheimer's
  disease--Patients--New Mexico--Biography. | Alzheimer's
  disease--Patients--Family relationships--New Mexico.
Classification: LCC RC523.2 F67 2021 | DDC 362.1968/3110092 [B]--dc23
LC record available at https://lccn.loc.gov/2020057873

WWW.SUNSTONEPRESS.COM
SUNSTONE PRESS / POST OFFICE BOX 2321 / SANTA FE, NM 87504-2321 /USA
(505) 988-4418 / FAX (505) 988-1025

CONTENTS

PREFACE

Life is not a smooth flowing continuum. Things happen unexpectedly, randomly and out of order. There are surprises, gifts, disappointments, even tragedies. The low points are devastating but are often redeemed by what follows—eventual recovery, new beginnings. Our lives have a central narrative, but the road is not straight and predictable. Family and daily routine provide continuity and comfort. New people add spice and texture. The roundabouts and detours can be meaningful and provide distraction, short-term escapes, and changing environments. The ebb and flow of highs and lows is usually within a range that can be tolerated and accommodated, but there are some blindsiding blows that knock us off course. For my Chris and for me, it was Alzheimer's.

In our case, it was impossible to know how the Alzheimer's patient perceived the disease as she lived through the years of suffering and decline. She denied her condition until late in its progress and couldn't describe her experience of its symptoms. We could only surmise her subjective awareness by what she revealed through her behavior and demeanor. But my experience of the disease as a caregiver, husband, and lover is something that lends itself to description.

As an escape and sometimes cathartic therapy, I kept notes and occasional journal entries, tracking our shared journey and providing a record of contemporaneous reactions to the injury she and we were suffering. There are great dissimilarities from patient to patient in how the disease expresses itself and how victims progress through the stages of the long decline. Some victims are gentled and accepting. Others are angry, even violent and resistant. My Chris trended toward the latter extreme, but for us, it was not an unmitigated hell.

While dealing with the intrusive impact of her illness, there were happy times for her, me, our children, and grandchildren, all of whom were spectators and participants in the drama. We were often able to be distracted and entertained by the other aspects of life and could celebrate the good things and agonize over the disasters in the world around us. And there were also good times for her along the way. Much later, we also learned that we survivors could, with time, recover. When the ordeal was over for her and for us, we grieved deeply but gradually came to see there was light at the end of the tunnel, however dim it was in the early days. My loss was most intense, as it should have been, but slowly a new world emerged to recapture my optimism and hope.

Both during and after the Alzheimer's siege, many of our days were brightened by a little-known place called Santa Rita, on the far northern edge of New Mexico. We had acquired a piece of land along a little river, the Rio de Los Pinos. The property included a rustic old cabin built by the original homesteader. It was an antique architectural design, called Jacál, in the local vernacular, with external walls of vertical, side by side posts rising to ceiling level, originally plastered with adobe mud, inside and out, and topped with a pitched tin roof. Years later, Baudelio Garcia, my friend and neighbor, and I worked together to build a straw bale cabin that became our beloved part time home in the valley. The cabins and the place are central characters in this story. Baudelio taught me much of what I know of the Hispano homeland and its people. In the last tortured years of Chris's life, his friendship and the place where we came together softened her pain and mitigated my loss.

Santa Rita Canyon

The Shadow of Things to Come

We've just put Chris in that damn memory care jail and there's a big hole in my life. She's still here but she's gone. I'm torn between relief and grief, mostly grief today. It's a night at the cabin, first time since it happened. I'm sitting on the porch with an empty chair beside me. The empty chair is hard to deal with as I recall the hundreds of times we have been here together. Still, I don't have second thoughts ... or do I? It was the right thing to do, for her, for me, but sitting here with that empty chair and the empty bed I will move to soon, it's hard to be satisfied with having made the right decision.

Christine Mason Flint was my wife and partner for sixty years, and our time together was mostly grand for fifty-four of those years. Times were increasingly challenging and agonizing for the last six.

At the beginning of those last years, she was the same vital person she had always been, just pleasantly older. She still had the sharp wit, self-confidence, and strongly held values and opinions she always had. She was still devoted to me and her family and always ready with a quick smile or a sarcastic challenge. Her once brown hair had long since turned grey, but she was one of those people who looked great in grey. We were good together and life was good. Then, almost imperceptibly, those qualities began to slip away, occasionally and cyclically. One day fine, the next day a mystery. As is commonly the case, many years passed as we made the gradual, inevitable, irreversible journey from there to here, and for the survivors, beyond.

Our life had been full and satisfying. We did the special, long delayed things people look forward to in retirement. We traveled to England several times to visit our son and his soon-to-be wife, and we saw old friends there from my days of employment. We visited Scotland, Ireland, France, Italy, and Spain. Back home, we skied together for years, a challenge Chris accepted bravely since I loved the sport. She even acquiesced when I pursued a lifelong fantasy and worked briefly as a ski instructor, teaching mostly "never ever" beginners. I was the only instructor insured both by workers' compensation and Medicare. Our Santa Fe social circle was small and comprised mostly of old friends, a circle that slowly shrank as the years passed. All the things we did, we did together, and in those last six years, her increasing limitations narrowed the scope of our activities.

Another constant in our life was the old cabin on the land we had acquired in partnership with Santa Fe friends, decades before. The Hispano locals called the place Santa Rita, a name given to it by the first settlers, who began to create a tenuous community there at the end of the nineteenth century. The place and our neighbors there expanded our life experience and gave us the gift of friendship with Hispano people and exposure to their culture that would not otherwise have been easily accessible to Anglo outsiders.

Our property was one of a few in-holdings of private land along the river, surrounded by the Carson National Forest and the Cruces Basin Wilderness. Santa Rita had been a tiny farming and ranching community. The pioneers were drawn there by the Rio de Los Pinos, which was the source of their subsistence livelihood. In the words of an old Spanish proverb, "El agua es la vida," water is life. It was what drew the pioneers to the place and without the river it would have been impossible to make a living there. The pattern of settlement in New Mexico had always been driven by water. The early people followed the rivers north, seeking out the places where they could take water from the small Rio Grande tributaries, irrigate the meadows, water and feed their animals and use the precious liquid for their domestic needs.

The contemporary journey to this place provides a hint of how remote and inaccessible it was when they came here. Travelling north from Santa Fe, there are two alternate routes to Santa Rita, the choice being dependent on the season, the weather and the impulse of the driver. The "high road," takes one six miles across the state line to Antonito, west four miles to Mogote, then south over the high ridge between Colorado's Conejos River and New Mexico's Rio de Los Pinos and finally down a rough Forest Service road to our gate. The "low road" heads west from the interstate highway just north of the state line, back south and up the valley of the Rio de Los Pinos, through the tiny villages of Ortiz, Colorado, and San Miguel and Los Pinos, New Mexico, and finishes with a primitive three-mile long Forest Service road to our neighborhood. Either route takes forty-five minute from the main road. One can only imagine the journey in a horse and buggy or a Model-T Ford in the early 1900s.

When we arrived, only Baudelio, his wife, Arlene and their two children continued to live there and work the land. His elderly parents, Antonio and Juanita still used their old adobe house next door to us, on a seasonal basis. Baudelio and Arlene had started their married life living in the valley year-round without electricity or running water. When Chris and I met them, they had moved their principal residence over the northern ridge, across the state line, and down the other side to the little village of Mogote, Colorado, where they could begin to live a more twentieth century life. He continued to manage the acequias, harvest the hay, and graze his cows and calves along the river on his land and ours in Santa Rita. They still occasionally used their Santa Rita cabin. He was one of twelve children who grew up in the house where he was born. Two of his great- grandfathers were among the original homesteaders in Santa Rita and had helped shape it to what we encountered when we came on the scene

When Chris and I first met him, he was a handsome young man in his thirties, not a tall man but he always stood tall. Whether on a horse, a tractor, in his pickup, or on his ATV, his posture was always perfect and his bearing almost military. A man of few words, he was dignified and reticent but warm and friendly. Spanish was his first language and he was cautious and sparing in his English conversation. His warm, brown face was weathered by years in the dazzling New Mexico sun. He had dark curly hair and enjoyed varying his facial hair style from week to week. His smile was easy and wide, displaying beautiful white teeth that originated in a Mexican dental facility in the border city of Juarez. He was a small man but strong as a horse, ready to toss bales and calves during the annual branding season.

The old homestead house we acquired was a primitive, three-room "shotgun" structure built over a hundred years ago by the original homesteader, Juan Bautista Gallegos. We shared the cabin with our co-owners, gradually making it more habitable, until 1995, when Baudelio and I partnered to build a straw bale cabin for our family. The time we spent with the Garcias over the years and working together with Baudelio on the cabin building project strengthened our relationship and enhanced the appreciation Chris and I had for the larger community of which we were becoming a part.

The new cabin became a dominant feature in our life and deserves a more

The Old Cabin - 1977

complete introduction. After sharing the old cabin for years—the Kelly week, the Smith week, our week—the Flints were restless to have a place of our own. Our partners were happy to consider having one less set of residents in the old place, and it was agreed we could carve out a new building site on our shared acreage. We wanted the new structure to be a handmade cabin but were challenged to come up with a design that would be realistically achievable. We examined the options—adobe bricks, logs, frame stucco—and concluded that from a practical and aesthetic standpoint, they were not right for our skill level or appropriate for the place. My carpentry skills, if they can be dignified with that term, reached their peak level when I was in my seventh-grade shop class, fifty years before. My enthusiasm had to be tempered with self-awareness. The quandary was resolved with the magical discovery of a book on straw bale construction. The author had faced a challenge like ours as she looked for a building solution that would be "fast, easy, warm, and inexpensive." Her book made a convincing case for straw bales, saying they were "super energy efficient, simple to work with, and can be used both inexpensively and aesthetically." We were hooked.

A Santa Fe straw bale professional turned our rough floor plans into working drawings. In addition to the above attractions of straw bales, the thick walls and adobe colored stucco finish would make the cabin aesthetically compatible with the local architectural tradition. By the ensuing spring, we were ready to roll but knew we needed helping hands. We turned to Baudelio. Like me, he had no experience with straw bales but had great common sense, a wealth of problem solving experience, and he was the owner of a tractor, a front end loader and back hoe, and a road grader, all things we would need to prepare the site and complete the ambitious project.

Garcia family in front of Santa Rita home in 1954 when Baudelio (second from left) was 13.

Straw is the byproduct or waste from harvesting grains, such as wheat, barley, or oats. The mature stalks are cut in the field and processed with a threshing machine, or combine, that separates the seed or grain from the stalks. The remnant straw is usually baled and used for a variety of purposes, including erosion control in highway projects, bedding for animals, and surprisingly, for building construction. Unlike hay, straw has no nutritional value and is not appealing to mice and other critters. Straw bales and hay bales look very much the same, except straw is more yellow than hay. Hay bales are derived from alfalfa or other grasses, cut and dried in the field, baled, and used for animal feed.

Our cabin is a post and beam structure, built on a concrete slab with plumbing and electrical elements embedded in the slab. The straw bales were shaped and stacked in the spaces between the posts to create the exterior walls. Chicken wire was stretched over and firmly attached to the bale walls, and plaster or stucco was applied to the inside and outside of the exterior walls. The exterior dimensions of the house are forty-six feet by twenty-seven feet, with an eight-foot-wide roofed porch across the front. The house has a Pro-Panel pitched metal roof, and heat is provided primarily by a very efficient wood cookstove, from Waterford, Ireland. As the book predicted, building with straw was easier and cheaper than it would have been with conventional materials. The house also has remarkable insulation quality, three times that of conventional exterior wall systems. This physical description doesn't begin to tell the story of the building experience or the memories of the summer and fall of 1995. Working with Baudelio provided us with the gift of meeting neighbors, shop keepers, artisans and extended families that enhanced the experience of working and living in close proximity to the San Luis Valley of Colorado.

Preparations began in the early spring. Chris and I met with Baudelio and Arlene to work out our compensation relationships. It is difficult to negotiate such things with friends, but we did it in a businesslike way. We agreed he would be paid $45 an hour when operating his mobile equipment. When I asked him what he should be paid for his labor, he gave it some thought and answered, "Well, when I work for the highway department, they pay me eight dollars an hour and I don't have to work too hard, so eight dollars will be fine." We had a deal. After the snow was mostly off the fields, Baudelio, Chris, and I ambled over the site we had selected and paced out the approximate outline of the foundation. At the beginning of June, we began to level the site, using the road grader and frontend loader. Much of the earth moving and leveling had to be done with shovels and other hand tools. It was a tough, time-consuming process.

Our progress through the summer and fall was long, slow, and deliberate. We were learning on the job. We made intuitive decisions, reading between the lines of the cryptic working drawings. There were many starts and stops along the way, but by late October, the walls were up, the doors and windows were installed, the roof was on, and we spent our first night camping out in the unfinished interior, warmed by the fire in our wonderful wood stove. There was much remaining to be done, but we were well on our way.

It's impossible to encapsulate the experience of that year in a few words, but it was life-changing for Chris and me. It deepened our connection with Baudelio and Arlene as we marinated in and absorbed the flavor of the Hispano culture we were surrounded by for those intense months. Chris and I had been committed working partners in our marriage, but in the earlier years we had complementary but different roles. I worked outside the home in an office. She managed the home, our finances, and had a greater responsibility for raising our children. That summer and fall provided our first extended experience of working shoulder to shoulder on the same job. We came out of that time closer and more connected than ever before.

From the beginning of this unfamiliar task, we were like the little engine that could, telling ourselves, "I think I can. I think I can." When I had doubts, Chris said, "You can do it. We can do it." When she worried about the cost, I said, "It will be less than you think. We can afford it." And as we hunted and chased down things we needed and people who could assist us, Baudelio was our guide, helping us navigate the largely Hispano neighborhood and making things work. For example, we were shopping for straw bales in the spring, the time of the year when they were most in demand and least available. You can't build a straw bale house

Chris on porch

without straw bales, and we were running out of ideas. After a fruitless search in Alamosa, Colorado, Baudelio dropped by after dinner one evening and reported, "Good news. My friend Lionel Valdez up in Capulín has three hundred bales for a dollar fifty a bale. And he'll deliver!" It was a miracle.

Chris cooked for us and cared for us every day, bringing lunch to the building site from the old cabin and cold beer for us when we quit for the day. In the evening when I was studying the drawings and planning for the next day, there was always a nice dinner. She heated water for our outside shower so I could get a fresh start, sharing the shower with the mosquitos.

Most of our building supplies were provided and delivered by the La Jara Trading Post, a hardware store and lumber yard in the Colorado town by the same name. We often made the long trip there to pick up something we had forgotten to order. One day, Chris and I made the trip to buy six railroad ties to support one side of our porch. We had a cheerful visit with our friends and technical advisors there, and they loaded the ties on our truck. They were too long, so we had to leave the tailgate open. We drove carefully back to Antonito and stopped for something at the drugstore. When we pulled out from the curb, headed for Santa Rita, we saw a man chasing us down the street, frantically waving his arms. Chris said, "What the hell's that all about?" We slowed to a stop and he caught up with us and breathlessly said, "Your ties are in front of the drugstore. Sure enough, two ties were missing. We thanked him, went back to recover the damn ties, and cautiously headed home.

Baudelio's Arlene was tiny; barely five feet tall and weighing not much more than a hundred pounds, but she had been a truck driver in her youth before earning teaching credentials at Adams State College in Alamosa, and she was stronger than she looked. She told us her father was a "red Indian." She couldn't provide more specific information on his tribal connection because she really didn't know. He could have had Ute or Navajo blood lines. He also could have been what is known as a *genízaro*, a group of people of mixed blood or detribalized Indians, captured during seventeenth- and eighteenth-century raids by both Hispanos and Indians and sold into slavery by both peoples. Arlene's own facial features suggested that she might have come from that background. When we asked her where her people came from, Arlene's answer was, "We've always been here." She may have been right about that.

One day in early September, Baudelio and I were installing seventeen-foot-long metal roof panels. I was on a tall extension ladder, holding the panels in place. Baudelio was on the roof, screwing the panels to the roof joists. There was thunder in the area and gentle rain began to fall. I said, "Baudelio, we need to get off of here." He said, "Let's finish this last panel." I said, "It's going to get slippery." He responded, "I'm almost done." Then he started slipping, skidding slowly down toward me. I braced myself and tried to stop his slide. It didn't work. We tangled and toppled; my ladder went one way and I fell to the ground. He went the other way and fell ten feet, landing on his back and barely missing some big rocks. Miraculously, we both popped back up unhurt, and I said, "I hope Chris didn't hear that." She did. She came around the corner and said, "What the hell's going on here?" I said, "We heard the thunder and decided to come down." Baudelio added, "We came down the fast way." After all these years, I still can't believe neither of us was injured.

One early October morning, Chris decided to stand on a small, low table to reach and clean the top of the refrigerator in the old cabin. The table collapsed and she fell to the floor in severe pain, clutching her left foot. I feared it was broken and tried to comfort her as she lay on the floor. I removed her shoe, and we waited for the pain to subside a bit. I was devastated and in disbelief. She cried and said, "Oh shit. I don't think I can get up. I can't believe I did that." We waited and I worried. I was finally able to get her up, and with her arm around my shoulder, managed to get her into the truck and recline the seat back. Fighting back her tears and between sobs, she lamented, "Everything was going so great and now I've really screwed things up." Like a good husband, I tried to reassure her with the usual lie, "Everything is going to be okay."

We slowly made our way up the rough forest service road out of the valley and on over to the Conejos County Hospital in La Jara, Colorado. It's a small facility with limited services, but we managed to get X-rays that showed she had broken bones in her foot. They were unable to do anything further for her there and recommended we seek treatment in Santa Fe. We made the sad drive home, put her to bed, and the next morning took her to an orthopedic doctor. He confirmed there were four broken bones, fitted her with a soft cast, and told us she would just have to avoid putting weight on the foot until it had healed. With crutches and a wheelchair, she gamely came back to the cabin with me that weekend. She tried to help, but it was no place for an injured patient, and she was miserable. We were both depressed and disappointed that the injury would require her to stay most of the time in Santa Fe, depriving us of the fun of working together through the next stages of the project.

Her injury and partial incapacity reminded me again how much I relied on her support. We had enjoyed a happy and satisfying life together for decades, not without challenges and setbacks, which we survived in large part because of her toughness, tenacity, and wisdom. Her down-to-earth common sense often provided answers I couldn't see with my more analytical approach to problem solving. I overthought things, and she gently reproached me. When I apologized one time for my shortcomings, I recall her saying, "It was worse when we were young, and you didn't even know how to fry an egg." In fact, I did know how but like many men of my vintage, I just didn't admit it.

We survived the unfortunate interruption and continued our project through the late summer and into the fall. We managed to move into the unfinished *casita* in late October. I had recovered Chris from Santa Fe where she had been convalescing from her broken foot. When we arrived, the house was cold and filthy as indoor plastering had been the latest milestone. We were rescued by an invitation for dinner with Baudelio and Arlene at their cabin, just down the road. It was a warm and comforting evening and the bottle of wine we enjoyed during the dinner allowed us to ignore the state of our new home and get a good night's sleep. We soldiered on into late November when the last visit by our commuting plumber gave us our first hot shower in the new cabin, a climactic event in the long adventure of turning our long endeavor into a new home.

In the long years of our cabin visits, one of the unexpected pleasures was the trip itself, the two-hour-and-forty-five-minute commute back and forth from Santa Fe. The drive north was a salient part of the rhythm of our life, a scenic crescendo beginning with the soft notes of our familiar hometown, ascending through the middle register of the inelegant town of Española, the increasingly rural Hernandez, El Duende, and Ojo Caliente, then literally bursting up to the climax at the top of the high Taos Plateau, where mountains etched the sky in every direction. The encore was the slower final movement of our ramble up the increasingly rough and rustic road, along the river, to the cabin. The journey was always a treat to the eye, always different, with changing seasons and the weather.

Our trips in both directions often included a lunch stop at the Mesa Vista Café in Ojo Caliente. When we first began our regular trips north, we selected the Mesa Vista using our time-tested indicator of the best place for lunch in a small town. If there are a lot of pickup trucks out front, that's the place for good food and a warm

Chris in wheel chair, a temporary setback

welcome. The test was vindicated, and the place became a part of our life. It was open every day but Tuesday, from breakfast time until early evening. It was well into the third generation of family ownership, currently in the hands of Leonel and Monica Chacón.

It's a rustic place that grows on you sweetly like an old wisteria vine. The dining room is relaxed, with scattered tables of various vintages, some seating four, others up to eight. There's a low counter facing the kitchen with five handmade stools attached to the floor. The decorations are eclectic; lots of family and landscape photos telling part of the Chacón family story and depicting the surrounding neighborhood. There's a tiny antique wood cook stove, no longer in use, that now provides a display surface for antique household and farm appliances. The whole wall behind the counter is decorated with dozens of old iron objects, from horseshoes to all manner of tools. There's a huge stuffed seven-point elk head, ignoring the customers and looking longingly out the window at the forested hills.

The café has been operated by Leonel and Monica for who knows how long, and before that, by his father and mother and extended family. Monica is queen of the kitchen with cooking duties sometimes shared with her husband and other staff. Table service is provided by a shifting cast of family and friends from nearby and

Mesa Vista Cafe

19

as far away as El Rito, some twenty miles over the western mountains. First among equals, for me at least, is Veronica Chacón, whom I've known for years. Noticing her family name, I remember asking her once if she was an in-law. She replied, "No. I'm an outlaw." She was married to Leonel's brother. Among the others are Cindy and her daughter, Kaila, who sometimes cooks, Nora Bustos, her husband, Ricky, and her sister, Lloyda, who worked there before Nora joined the crew, (Lloyda was named after her uncle!). A variety of other young women from the Chacón family fill in from time to time.

The kitchen is the inner sanctum. It has an ancient wood cook stove, still working, as well as a propane stove. It's usually dominated by Monica, who because of her labors, is seldom seen out front, but there is a steady stream of people who go into the kitchen to pay their respects. Sometimes Leonel does the cooking, but even then, Monica is seldom seen out front. The menu is eclectic but leans toward New Mexico food, ranging from breakfast burritos to red or green enchilada plates.

Like many roadside cafes across the country, the Mesa Vista is a community gathering place. What makes this one distinctive is its Hispano character. Most of the people on both sides of the counter are products of the unique northern New Mexico culture that traces its roots back centuries to the first pioneers, some of whom came here as early as the late 1600s when this area was still ferociously contested by Native Americans. That confrontation meant that Ojo Caliente had a challenging start after the Spanish regained control of their New Mexico colony following the Pueblo Revolt of 1680. Ojo was on the front lines of community building efforts, the Spanish settlers advancing and retreating as the Navajos and Utes resisted the newcomers. There are gun ports high up on the walls of the old church, evidence of the fragile, defensive nature of the settlement.

The café is a welcoming place with a cast of regulars but often hosts visiting patrons who no longer live nearby, but who stop when passing through. The conversation is lively, often involving more than one table. Many among the majority Hispano customers generously include the Anglo newcomers and encourage wide ranging conversations that can go on long after the meals have been enjoyed. The locals welcome our interest in the culture and the community, and attesting to their loving respect for their shared language, they educate us and teach us new words, recalling anecdotes and history of the area.

Veronica Chacón

The "new cabin" on a fall afternoon

The regulars are enthusiastic to be our teachers and curious about our different life experiences. Through these lunchtime conversations, we learn things beyond what could be found in books, and we gain knowledge of the quirks and variances of the distinctive version of the Spanish language spoken by the Hispanos of northern New Mexico and southern Colorado.

Our frequent visits there had been an important part of our routine long before the onset of Chris's Alzheimer's. It seemed we often arrived in Ojo Caliente, going north or going south, just when it was "time for a little something," as Winnie the Pooh often declared. The Mesa Vista had provided pleasurable intermissions in our frequent journeys, but that and other pleasures began to be overshadowed by the noticeable changes in Chris. She was less animated and slower to engage in conversation. There were lapses in her short-term memory. We, her family and I, noticed what were at first only tiny mutations in her behavior. Each of us resisted what our senses told us and kept our concerns to ourselves. Perhaps two years after first seeing that evidence, I reluctantly shared my observations with my children. They confirmed their similar concerns. We quietly discussed our terrifying inklings. The phrase "short-term memory loss" entered our lexicon. Old stories began to be repeated, she lost track of recent events more often, and other signs emerged. Things were lost, even her partial plate. We searched for it for months without success. She began to put things in "safe places" she couldn't remember, and we couldn't divine.

Her vibrant personality lost its edge. At times she seemed to recover, and our hopes surged, but then things became worse again. She was more fearful, lost her self-confidence, was angry and frustrated more often, and resisted being in places and circumstances that were unfamiliar. She became my beloved Cheshire Cat, figuratively appearing and disappearing unpredictably. Sometimes she was sharp and focused. Other times she faded away, leaving us only with her enigmatic smile before reappearing as a more complete person. Like Lewis Carroll's Cheshire Cat, she sometimes told us that everyone in Wonderland was crazy, especially the wise doctor who took away her driver's license.

During the long months and years of our ordeal, Chris and I still often found the capacity to enjoy good times. We were usually alone because social interaction became more challenging and stressful. When in Santa Fe, we could still be out for lunch together, often at our beloved Shed Restaurant; a "Number 4, red enchilada" for her and a "Number 5, red enchilada with posole" for me. We were greeted with enthusiasm by Eric, the long-time front man. Eric had been there for what seemed like forever and became our friend. He's a big burly guy who lifts weights and anything else that needs lifting. At one point in those years, Chris fell and broke her hip. As she was recovering, I told Eric we hoped to get her back for lunch soon. He gave me a bear hug and said, "Just park out front and give me a signal. I'll come out and carry her ass in!"

In addition to a light social schedule in Santa Fe, we still spent a good part of the snow-free months at our cabin. During the early years of her illness, the solitude was comforting for her and for me. We enjoyed the trips back and forth, listening to music, admiring the giant view from high on the Taos Plateau looking across to the Sangre de Cristo Mountains, and struggling to find conversation. Three or four years into the deepening ravages of the disease, the therapeutic benefit of cabin escape was beginning to fade.

SPRING 2014

We're at the cabin and I'm putting words on paper, partly to record the passage of time but also to see if the passing days can teach me anything. I can record events such as they are and maybe find something beyond the ordinary to think about. Our life, Chris's and mine, seems to work better when we're here. She finds work to do, as she always does wherever we are, and having useful work to do is good therapy. It confirms your role as a productive person and makes a real contribution. Things feel better as a result. Today's work was a complete housecleaning; dusting and vacuuming the whole cabin and mopping the floors in the bathroom, hall, and main room. The sweet smell of Murphy's Oil Soap is a satisfying confirmation of the job well done. At 82, she's happily tired.

For me it was a day of spasmodic labor, none of it rationally prioritized. We have a wilderness cabin on an un-manicured piece of land along a wild river. The place doesn't cry out for meticulous landscaping, but the urge to do something useful is overwhelming, so I always find things to do.

But I'm beating around the bush. We're dealing with Alzheimer's here. And when it happens in your family, it is not a phenomenon on the edge of your consciousness. It becomes a constant character on the stage of your life; almost an additional person at the breakfast table, the lunch table, the dinner table, and all the other stops along the track of the day. In all my life, there has never been an issue so front-and-center all my waking hours every day. It's not an overwhelming factor most of the time, but it is a nagging irritant all the time. It's a full-time job. I want to manage our minutes and hours in a way that makes for the greatest comfort, happiness, and minimal stress for her. It's a guessing game. How is she feeling? She seems really with it this morning. Is she relaxed and cheerful or is she thinking about losing her driver's license? She seems warm and content with our relationship, but is she on the verge of depression and anger about the changes in her life?

It's late now after a great day. She did her work and I did mine. We had a lovely dinner, watched the valley darken, and felt the evening cool before we returned to our welcome, warm room. The house is spic and span, the outside as tamed as we want it. The birds and squirrels provided a full-time spectacle, and we have the calming impact of physical exhaustion. She relaxes with her eyes closed to the muted television, a routine feature of our existence. I'm winding down with the hope of a good rest and a happy morning. Gotta stay on my toes. Never know what the morning mood or message will be. Last glass of wine on the porch, a dark, lightly rainy evening. We don't get many of these in the high desert. It's cool enough now to enjoy a fire in the wood stove.

Good conversation after dinner; family stories, enjoying the warm fire and the sound of the river on the other side of the lush meadow. I could almost forget that our lives are compromised by the changes I try to ignore. Not quite. We move outside briefly, watch the scene disappear in the dusk. Bird sounds ramp down, leaving us with only the gentle rumble of the river. I tell her that where we are, up here on the northern boundary of New Mexico, is the best place of all places to be. She says, "Our home place in Santa Fe is also the best place to be"—a small sign of insecurity. I tell her I agree and say our home place is indeed a good place to be, but it doesn't have a river.

I remind her of the other best places of our life and begin to recall our changing geographic history. Storytelling often lubricates contentment. I tell her about that wonderful second-story apartment on Mesa Vista Street in Albuquerque, close to the university, where we returned after our wedding in Indiana; a place we soon couldn't afford when we had our first unexpected pregnancy with our Tina. She says, "I hated to leave that damn place." I continued, "Our next best place was the converted army barracks." It was housing for veterans provided by the University of New Mexico, where we lived in bliss until Tina's birth, sharing that $39-a-month place with other student families. That's me remembering. That's not what I told her. I reminded her of the favorite story of our simple metal shower stall and its shared backside with the shower in the next apartment, allowing Chris to have a morning conversation with our neighbor, Doug, while they showered. She said, "I remember that. Wonder what happened to Doug."

I went on: "Then we moved in with Roena." Roena was Chris's sister. We had a bedroom, a shared bath, and a shared life with a generous, caring woman who helped in many ways with the challenging, stimulating time when our new daughter took her first steps. I reminded her, even that important milestone was delayed by an early diagnosis of congenital hip dislocation that put Tina in a full body cast for months. Chris and I remembered that the cast, which reached up from her toes to her chin, restricted her physical movement but could not constrain her spirited joy with life. She said, "I remember her always smiling. I knew she was going to be a happy girl." I was recalling things for Chris but was really telling myself the story.

I rambled on, "After the final year of law school for me and school-teaching for you, we moved on to our next perfect place" (I was reminded that leaving Albuquerque for Santa Fe was a leap of faith for Chris, who was *more conservative than I was when it came to new places, but she adjusted and came to love it.) And then, "Our new best place was 909 Canyon Road" (a $75-a-month shotgun apartment in a very old adobe house, that featured occasional episodes of sand sifting down through the cracks in the ceiling onto the floor of our three-room home). "Do you remember how we loved that home? And that Harlan Myles was born while we were there?" She corrected me, "Of course I remember. Do you think I'm losing my memory?"*

That's where my story ended that night. She was very tired and could no longer keep up with my monologue on the history of our life. On to a good sleep for us both. I hoped.

THEN AND NOW

She was a small-town girl, the sixth of seven children. Her mother was one of three daughters of Seth Iden, who started The First State Bank out of his briefcase and later moved it into a proper bank building in Etna Green, Indiana. Having no sons, he enabled his daughter Mary Avis to attend Indiana University where she thrived, graduated, and was honored, some say, as a member of Phi Beta Kappa. Mary Avis, known as Avis, was Chris's mother. Seth could not have been described as a feminist, but unable to pass the bank along to sons, he ensured that his three daughters would become bankers, unusual occupations for women in that day.

Chris's father, Ralph Mason, was the son of Lewis Mason, owner of the local hardware store, and a respected businessman in their small town. Ralph made a stab at higher education at I.U. but was interrupted by a stint in the army during the First World War and never finished college. He married Avis, who prospered in her role as a bank manager, and on her father's death, should have become president of the bank. However, respecting the tradition that the president of a bank should be a man, she foreswore the title, yielding it to Bob Knepper. He had previously married her sister Amy, came to work in the family business, and now became its titular head.

Ralph Mason, seeing there was no room for another man in his wife's bank, went to work in and ultimately became the controlling owner and president of the Bourbon State Bank in the neighboring town. When in later years, Bob Knepper fell ill and died, Avis assumed her rightful role as president.

Chris grew up in a family with status. They were the big fish in a small pond. Her parents were successful in their separate endeavors, although they managed only modest financial rewards over the course of their working lives. Their two small banks survived the Great Depression that took down many community banks. They were ambitious for their children and undertook to make college available to any of them who had that goal.

Etna Green looked like many small towns in rural middle-America at that time—an unassuming commercial center surrounded by a busy agricultural region. Its growth was encouraged by the arrival of the railroad in the 1890s. The First

State Bank came into existence in a very informal way. Seth Iden used the train to visit clients in the even smaller town a few miles down the track, taking deposits and cashing checks along the way and wherever customers could be found. The first fixed location of the business was in the back of a drugstore. The first real bank building, across the street from the drugstore, was an ambitious brick building with a tall false façade making it look like a two-story structure.

The three sisters, all married with children by then, shuttled between the bank and their nearby residences sharing the responsibilities of bank managers with caring for children and managing their homes. These were hard times, in the middle of the Depression, and jobs were hard to come by. Homeless men—hobos they were called—frequently showed up at kitchen doors and were given food by the housewives. The Iden women lived modest lives but had the means to have "hired girls," often young women from the substantial neighboring Amish community, who came to work for and live with the host families. These girls earned room and board and a tiny financial payment for their services, making it possible for the Iden women to divide their time between bank and home.

Etna Green in the 1940s was a beehive of activity. There were several restaurants, at least two drugstores with soda fountains, three grocery stores, including Uncle Pete Hamlin's dominant establishment, a Ford dealership, several fully staffed garages, a pool hall, and other commercial establishments including the grain elevator and the train station. The Odd Fellows Hall was on the second floor over the Mason Hardware Store. There were three Protestant churches in town. On summer Saturday nights, the town was packed with shoppers in town to meet, greet, and share the activity and sociability.

That was the lively place where Chris spent her early years. Based on her recollections and my hearsay evidence from other family members, it seems she had a good and happy childhood, but her stories, especially in later life, seemed to focus on the downside. She often mentioned her disappointment that she had to wear glasses to see the blackboard. She vividly recalls being taunted and teased by the other children and called "four eyes." She was burdened by having to keep her hair long at her father's insistence, until he finally relented. Her long brown braid still exists in a box in a cupboard somewhere, together with a note recalling she was given permission to have it cut in 1949, when she was seventeen. She recalled her father coming to the shop while the deed was being done, looking on sadly, and leaving without a word. He lamented her lost childhood.

Her mother was an enigma. The family lore portrayed her as a remarkably liberated and independent young woman when she was in college. There are photos showing her smoking and drinking with her women friends, and there are stories of other modest rule breaking. Surely, she must have danced the Charleston, though we have no direct evidence. She was a serious and successful student following a diverse liberal arts curriculum. Unlike the other women at the University, she didn't use her years there as an avenue to marriage and came home after graduation unattached. The style she apparently displayed while off in Bloomington seems to have disappeared when she returned home.

She was private and inscrutable, seldom, in my experience, revealing who she really was and what she really thought. She was kind and loving in a restrained way, never made a display of her intellectual capacities, was modest about her academic success, and didn't easily reveal her inner self, at least in my presence. I can't recall hearing her express opinions on political or social issues, except away from home, perhaps most dramatically when she comfortably exchanged opinions with the Governor of Windsor Castle. Lord Elworthy was interested to hear about her experience running a small bank in Indiana and she seemed happy to describe the politics of her home state and community. The occasion for this unusual visit was a business trip to London for me. Chris, her mother and I enjoyed a memorable weekend at the Windsor Castle with the Governor and his wife. His role as the ceremonial protector of the queen while she was in residence at Windsor Castle provided him with a charming apartment in the Norman Tower. We remember him telling us, "It's a very old house, but it was completely modernized in the fifteenth century." We had been living in Alaska at the time of this trip, where I was an executive with BP America and had hosted Lord Elworthy on his recent visit there in his capacity as a Board member of the company.

Back in Indiana, Avis was a staunch Democrat but infrequently discussed politics or issues of the day. Despite her oral reticence, she was a dedicated correspondent with Chris, typewriting lengthy weekly letters, mainly reporting on daily happenings in Etna Green. Avis seemed to be a typical, conventional, Midwestern woman despite having been a lively, independent young woman, a successful university graduate, and a bank president. She deferred to the men in her family, first her husband and then her two older sons. She was a strong supporter of her local Christian church, attended faithfully, and saw that her children attended regularly. She was not outspoken about her beliefs and didn't press her views on her children, although while they were under her roof, they were expected to honor the family practices. I always hoped to break through her protective shield, but it never happened, and she slipped silently away without letting us know who she really was.

Chris frequently repeated the story about always being the "last one chosen for the kickball team" and was insecure and embarrassed by what she saw as her lack of athletic abilities. She also recalled that she "was not the cutest girl" in her class, though I think she was very cute. She stood about five foot five and was slim and energetic and as previously mentioned had long dark brown hair until she won the battle with her father and was allowed to cut it short It would be years before I met her but the photos from that time show her as a lovely, smiling teenager with lively, sparkling brown eyes, vigorous and outgoing and ready to take on the world.

She was clearly independent and a striver. As the sixth of seven children,

School portrait of Chris in 1946

she was low on the ladder of seniority, but she had a mind of her own and was no pushover. She already had the spunk and determination that would capture me in later years. She made up for what she saw as her shortcomings by committing herself to becoming the smartest kid in her classes, a striving that was always important to her. She didn't take herself too seriously and had what could be described as an unvarnished sense of herself, a cool, dispassionate way of looking at the world and her own capacities. In later years, she described this perspective by saying, "I'm a realist." That said, she was tough, strong, and had the will to overcome significant obstacles with a fighter's resilience and spunk. Her independence and staunch tenacity were even foretold by remarks in her baby book written by her somewhat distressed mother.

> *Christine was a very cross baby .... By August she was somewhat better ... but was never a <u>good</u> baby.*

> *Christine was too cross to take away from home until January 1933.*

> *She was apparently a stray sheep as to her appearance and her disposition as well, as she was always belligerent and strong-willed.*

In some ways, Chris was her mother's daughter. She admired and emulated her mother's educational achievement. She honored and adopted her mother's values of basic decency and integrity. She deviated from her mother's life pattern with her stern commitment to defining her own course in life. She was a fighter. She avoided following the path of least resistance. If she had followed her mother's path, she could easily have been trapped in a more conventional life, returning to and accepting her youthful physical and cultural environment.

After her death, as I struggled to discover the Chris who existed before I met her, I turned to the cardboard boxes full of a lifetime of documents and pictures that contained hints of her history. As I sorted the long-ignored archives, I came across her diary for the years 1944 and 1945, when she was an early teenager. The small leather-bound diary was locked, and when I snipped the leather strap that protected her privacy, I was met with a stern rebuke: "Keep your damn nose out of this. Is this any of your business?" Undaunted, I pressed on. It was a treasure trove, often about boys and discovering they could not always be trusted.

We took Jim home. He wanted to kiss me, but I wouldn't let him.

Saw Bill. He called me up and asked me for a date. I'm gonna go. Yippee!

Went to tourney with Bill. Sure wish I was going with Jim. Bill's nice, but Jim's nicer. Dammit!

Bill's funny sometimes. I don't know what the score is.

Crapped around. Went to ballgame at Tippy. We beat. Mack, Jim, and Bill came. We sat around and told dirty jokes through the game.

Sometimes there were dates for the entries.

May 19. NOTHING?!

June 19. June R. Huffer's expecting. Princess Elizabeth too!!!

June 25. Listened to fight. Joe Louis still champ.

August 14. War over in Japan. Announced at 6:00 p.m.

November 2. School is crummy. Got straight A's.

November 4. Same old Bill. Just meandered over, and we went out and molly-gobbed. I must admit I've got a bad case of "it."

December 23. Haven't seen Jim for ages. I'll always go with him, but I'm through hunting him.

December 28. Went to dance with Bill. He can kiss better than anyone else. Hubba Hubba!!

Even before I was privileged to see her diary, Jimmy Dillingham and Billy Becknell were household names in our home. I remember Chris telling me that their mothers loved her and always tried to cook her favorite food whenever she was there for dinner. She didn't take the bait.

I should be quick to add that what I have extracted from the diary so far doesn't do justice to the other things she described that helped make her the person she became. Over and over she mentioned the uncounted hours spent doing the work required in a large middle-class family home; washing, ironing, house cleaning, gardening, canning, harvesting, and all the other jobs that kept things going. Not surprisingly, the girls seemed to be doing most of the work. She devoted much time tending Aunt Marjorie, her father's sister, who suffered from heart disease that couldn't be repaired in those days. Marjorie spent much of her youthful final days bedridden and dependent on the kind of care that is unavailable in most families today.

There were frequent mentions of going to "S.S.," which I finally realized referred to Sunday School. The church obligation was obviously a recurring element of the rhythm of life. There was never any mention of the substance of this weekly ritual, suggesting that this part of her life didn't have a deep impact on her religious perspective. In our later life together, we had few conversations about her thoughts and beliefs as a child, or even as an adult for that matter. She was not openly introspective, and like her mother, not inclined to reveal her inner self. She seemed comfortable with the tolerant convictions of the Unitarian church where we spent our spiritual intervals during the child raising years.

Her years at Indiana University nourished her independent streak, despite paternalistic counsel from her older brother that might have dampened her ambition. Chris loved journalism but knew the employment prospects were limited. She also loved history, but her big brother discouraged that major, telling her that the professors in the history department might be too challenging for her. Since she was a self-described realist, she decided to earn teaching credentials, a career objective she knew was available to women. While meeting the soporific requirements to be certified, she also managed to have double majors in Spanish and English, choices that prepared her not only for employment but for a fulfilling and rich life.

The university years provided other benefits. Her early family instruction in tolerance and openness to people of different backgrounds was reinforced by her social experience. She was exposed to ethnic and religious diversity not available in her hometown. She smoked, drank, danced, and had romantic and social relationships with a mind opening variety of interesting people of diverse religious and ethnic shades. There were Hungarian and Ukrainian friends, some of them Catholics and there was a Jewish boyfriend. Living in a sorority house, she enjoyed the stimulating camaraderie of likeminded friends, but often preferred the company of the more socially diverse houseboys who served their meals and lived in the basement. During the pledge process, she is remembered for raising strong protest when sisters threatened to use their blackball veto to deny membership for frivolous or discriminatory reasons.

Many women friends saw the college years as preparation not for employment but for marriage. They often married right after receiving their diplomas or even before. During the college years, Chris had enjoyed a boyfriend or two but never made a binding commitment. She had opportunities but had the good sense to know that some of her suitors were more interested in the possibility of sex than in serious commitment. She was firm in her decision to not let that happen. She wanted more life experience, the time to enjoy her freedom, and the right man hadn't come along. She was content to bide her time and live to make a better decision later. That was my good fortune.

···

Back to the harsh reality of her affliction, I pondered our uncertain future, shadowed by the specter of the progressing disease, I often looked back with nostalgia at the good times. Those memories provided temporary relief from the demands of the day and restored me to deal with what lay ahead. As a family, we took it a step at a time, trying not to focus exclusively on the end game. There were many family conversations, shared observations, advice, and support. The world was shrinking for Chris and me, causing us to live more of our time in the narrow confines of our house in Santa Fe and our cabin.

With the constraints of our circumstances, it was necessary for me to find other outlets. Chris was no longer able to join me for skiing, an activity that had occupied an important part of our winter lives. For a while, I was able to leave her for half a day of skiing alone, but as she became more insecure, I was phasing out of that escape. We belonged to a gym and frequently went there after breakfast to follow the programs designed by our trainer. Chris could enjoy that time with me, but she began to be less able to remember the sequence of exercises and was frustrated by the need to have assistance.

Our doctor's decision that she should no longer be driving hit Chris like a death sentence, and the delivery of that sentence was awkward and painful. After telling us of her decision, the doctor ungracefully contacted the motor vehicle department and cancelled the license without advising Chris or me she was doing so. When we received the revocation notice from the state department, I was left with the task of delivering the verdict to Chris. Not surprisingly, it was devastating news, a trauma that cast a dark shadow for the rest of her life. She was angry, resentful, and deeply hurt by the loss of freedom. She hated our doctor who had cared for us both for years. Chris often said with fervor and a sense of betrayal, "She's never seen me drive. I've never had an accident. How can she do this to me? I hate her." That became a constant refrain for the rest of her days.

I had occasionally been the passenger when she was the driver and had been looking for signs that she was at risk. She had always been a good driver and still seemed to be competent, but was she too close to the curb? Did she use the turn signal? We are all backseat drivers at times, and I questioned my observations of her slight shortcomings. Then she had a small contact with another car while backing up at the bookstore. The other driver generously shared the blame and I tried to put it behind me. Then one day she drove too close to a roadside trash can and struck and broke the rearview mirror. My heart sank. I knew it was time for her to stop driving but dreaded it since she would see it as a symbol of the approaching end. In a sense, the doctor's graceless action relieved me from having to make the fateful decision. But for her, it would always be "the goddamn doctor."

Our time at the cabin became more challenging. We often planned for a three-day visit only to find that on the morning of the second day, she would be anxious to "go home." Sometimes I could tempt her to stay, finding projects to divert her or by taking a quick trip "to town," Antonito, to pick up unneeded groceries. My schemes sometimes worked. Other times they didn't, and we would be obliged to make the forlorn drive back to Santa Fe. One of those occasions was a fall day about two years before the end of her ordeal. Our Sunday afternoon had been reasonably unthreatening until she tried to help me with dinner preparation and about drove me over the edge with well-intentioned but counterproductive suggestions.

Our time after dinner was comforting. I read, and we listened to music. One selection was from an Oscar Peterson album and included a lovely cut she enjoyed. She said, "I want that played at my funeral." I nodded but had no response. A bit later, she repeated the request. It was the first time I can recall that she seemed to acknowledge and confront her fate, and I tried to comfort her and refocus her attention. The next morning, her first words were, "I'm depressed," and soon after that she said, "I want to get out of here." Obviously, her mood was as it had been the previous evening, and I was depressed for her and for me. We had planned to stay for another day, and we had always been reluctant to leave early. It was clear that her focus would not change, so we packed up and headed down the road. She was teary and said, "I'm sorry to make you leave, and if you want to stay, it's okay with me." But I knew it was best to leave. It made me doubly sad to see that she was driven to get away but also had the pain of recognizing that her fear and compulsion were not rational.

One August evening we managed to stay, and we were rewarded by seeing four cow elk and about the same number of calves. They filtered down out of the trees on the hillside, crossed the meadow, calves frolicking, the cows more cautious. Rainy, cold weather had kept most of the "tourists" away. My friend Chris Garcia, told me that the Hispanos called the Anglos "tourists" even if they had been property owners here for many years.

My Chris said, "You're very quiet tonight. Are you okay? I responded ambiguously, "I'm fine. Just a little tired, I guess." Conversation was becoming more challenging. There were fewer things to talk about, but that night we found a useful subject. I'm not sure how it came up, but we talked about cultural differences and the effect they have on relationships. She described vivid memories of sitting in her first-grade classroom; Christine Mason, and right behind her, seated alphabetically, was Chester Mast, an Amish boy. Chris remembers that he was cute and smart. She said, "I liked him. He was nice most of the time, but sometimes he pulled my braid." Chester, like most Amish children, was destined to drop out of school as soon as it was legal. She recalls him as an important figure in her early life because his presence introduced the realization that the larger world included people who were different. She later commented that many people don't experience "others" until they are older.

The other "others" in her life were the Appalachian neighbors who came up to Indiana from the mountains, mostly from Kentucky. In the local lingo, those people were stereotypically referred to as "KYs." They were often poor, spoke a different dialect, and were less likely to be landowners like the Amish, putting them two rungs down the social ladder from the local majority. She doesn't recall her parents teaching the children about how they should treat these others, but they were clearly raised to be tolerant.

Chris as a young bride

Chris's small town was uniformly Christian, with three different Protestant versions of the faith, all quite similar in their teaching to my untutored eye. It seems unlikely that the churches dealt seriously with the issue of diversity, and even the Amish were an exotic part of the Christian family. I remember Chris telling me that when she was young and her mother was discussing their Amish neighbors, she said, "They are our Negroes." I can't confidently interpret her use of that phrase but believe she didn't mean it in a pejorative sense. It's more likely she saw the Amish as being disadvantaged and discriminated against, in a way similar to that of African Americans. That said, there is little doubt that those in the majority in her community considered themselves to have higher social ranking than the Amish and certainly, the KYs.

What I took away from our conversation was that, even in her damaged state, Chris was adamant that she didn't share that bias. She didn't feel superior to others based on their ethnic, racial, or social status, and that is borne out by everything I knew from our decades of shared time together.

On one of our autumn stops at the Mesa Vista, we joined Tony Chacón at his regular table. The place is like the coffee houses of old. People are there for food and conversation. Prominent among them was Tony. He's a native of the region and is a regular at the restaurant, always there on Wednesdays but frequently more often. He's a storyteller. Some of his stories recount the ordinary things of daily life, but others verge on folklore. Despite living over the hill in El Rito, he has found his place in the diverse crowd that gathers for the midday ritual in Ojo Caliente. The participants assemble without formal plans, whenever chance brings them together to enjoy good food and lively conversation. Over time, that eclectic group of people become friends and looked forward to these meetings as an important part of their days.

Tony's tales often grew out of his early life in rural northern New Mexico, a place where imagination and magic fill the empty spaces of reality. Conversation is the lubricant that puts thoughts into spoken words. Some of the magic derives from the Catholic faith that encourages a ready belief in miracles and allows the mind to accept as rational and believable events that would otherwise be dismissed as incredible. Beyond that, the Hispano culture of the north is enriched by myth and legend, bringing to life and lending credibility to the supernatural.

One day while lunching with Tony and Jamie Ross, our poet and artist friend from the even smaller village of Carson, Tony recounted a tale related to work he did many years ago in the general area of White Sands Missile Range, a secret military facility in southern New Mexico. He was employed by a technical government contractor. They had been called out to help with a problem dealing with a top-secret semi-trailer that was found parked along a remote roadside in the wilds of that region. When they arrived, the body of the trailer was open, split down the middle, with each side lowered outward to the ground, supported by giant hinges. The problem was that the hinges had buckled under the weight and stress of the two halves of the trailer roof and the two sides couldn't be lifted. Tony was startled to see a huge telescope in the bed of the trailer that could be raised to make heavenly observations wherever the vehicle was parked.

While they were discussing the problem, one of the engineers whispered to Tony that he was about to be a witness to a top secret happening and warned him to not show any surprise. He was sworn to protect the confidentiality of what he would see. Immediately thereafter, there was a roar in the distance and two military jets appeared, streaking across the sky, one behind the other, seemingly headed for a horrendous collision with the craggy mountain to their front. To his shock and amazement, just as the first jet seemed certain to disintegrate on impact, an opening appeared in the mountainside and the first plane disappeared into the hole, followed instantly by the second. Just as quickly as the apparent door opened, it closed behind the two jets. There was no sound or visible sign of a crash, and the place where the mountain had opened appeared once again like the undisturbed surface of the cliff.

As he looked on in disbelief, the mysterious doorway reopened, and the two aircraft raced out of the mountain in single file and quickly disappeared over the horizon. Tony thought to himself that the military had built an amazing underground landing strip inside the mountain and that a successful, out of sight landing and takeoff had occurred right before his eyes. Tony told the story with complete seriousness and convincing sincerity. We listeners withheld any sign of skepticism or disbelief and shared our amazement at the magical events Tony had observed.

Before we could gather our thoughts or test his tale with questions, Tony launched into another story, this one dating back to his young years growing up in El Rito when he spent much of his time in the larger neighborhood of the Los Alamos Nationals Laboratory and the Sandia Lab in Albuquerque. During and after the Second World War, the two labs were shrouded in secrecy and plagued with rumor and suspicion about what happened in those well-guarded and mysterious places. Many people from Española, El Rito, Chimayo, and other small communities worked in Los Alamos without really knowing what was going on there but carrying home their speculation about its inner workings.

There had been widespread conviction among the workers that there was an unobserved but constant interchange and movement of people, materials, and information between the facilities in Albuquerque and Los Alamos. Tony and other young people learned from older family members and friends who worked at the labs that the means by which this underground exchange was accomplished was literally underground. During the war, a secret tunnel had been constructed all the way between the two labs, allowing the exchange to take place without the knowledge of the general public.

This amazing deception had been sustained well into the twenty-first century and contributes even today to an unexplained phenomenon that baffled nongovernment scientists in recent decades. The phenomenon is known as the Taos Hum. For many years, ordinary people have experienced a low-frequency sound, often described as a hum, coming from an unknown source. The direction from which the sound emanates is hard to verify, but for some reason it seems to be heard most distinctly in the greater Taos region. Geologists and other scientists have studied the mystery for decades, and many theories have been explored, but no satisfactory answer has emerged.

However, the convincing folk wisdom of the people of El Rito, supported by folks in other rural districts in the north, tells us that the so-called Taos Hum is caused by the still occurring flow of vehicles, materials, and electronic data through the secret tunnel between our two atomic research labs. That was Tony's tale, and who were we to dispute it?

These stories are just the tip of the iceberg. Magical realism is alive and well in the hills, mountains, and villages of New Mexico's ancient Hispano homeland.

...

My obvious preoccupation with things Spanish may deserve further explanation. It began when I was in the ninth grade in a small progressive boarding school on a rural hillside in Vermont. I was born in the small state of Rhode Island, a diverse microcosm of early twentieth century America, by faith comprised mostly of Catholics, Protestants and Jews. Most of them came from northern and southern European countries. There were a very few Asians and a slightly larger number of African Americans. New England Yankees were at the top of the social pecking order, heirs of the original white, protestant folk, many of whom claimed ancestors who had arrived on the Mayflower.

The Putney school, where I spent my first two years of high school, aspired to host a student body drawn from a miniscule sample of the globes' variety of cultures, including a small number of students from the western hemisphere diaspora of the Hispanic World. One school mate was from the family of a famous Mexican artist. And then there was Mara Moser. She was the amazing teacher who introduced a handful of us to Spain and the Spanish language. I put it that way because she taught the language in the context of the culture from which it derived. We soon came to know that she was a refugee from Spain who had suffered from the latest version of the cyclical persecution of Jews that had marred the history of Spain for over a thousand years. We were naïve and unschooled but as children of the Second World War, we had some awareness of the Nazi's Jewish genocide we had learned of from afar. We were impressed that she had escaped the regime of General Francisco Franco and somehow found her way to a small school on a farm in rural Vermont.

She was a tiny, dark haired, middle aged woman, not imposing in stature, who spoke perfect English but with a charming accent. She had a magnetic quality that captured our attention. As a former Spanish citizen, she proudly spoke a Castilian version of the language and insisted from the outset that we repeat the words she gave us with perfection and respect for the proper sound of the spoken language.

She was dramatic and spoke with conviction that impressed and inspired us, to the extent that teenage kids can be in awe of anything an adult says. She managed to weave in elements of history and hints revealing the nature of Spanish life that were intriguing for us.

I was generally an uninspired student and inclined to be easily distracted from the task at hand but the force of her personality and her intense insistence that we accurately pronounce the ancient language reached me and left an indelible mark on this fourteen year old adolescent. She gave the language life and opened a window to its cultural context. I continued to study Spanish in my last two years of high school, back in Rhode Island, but without Mara Moser's inspiration.

My romance with the language and the culture was further enhanced by the graduation gift of two months in Spain. The adventure started with classes at the University of Madrid and the chance for me to meet ordinary citizens of the city, upgrade my conversational Spanish and marinate in the ambiance of the city. That was followed by two weeks in Andalusia that introduced the dramatic setting, atmosphere and landscape I would later learn was tantalizingly like that of northern New Mexico. The ancient city of Córdoba was ruled by Muslims for most of a millennium until they were expelled in 1498 by the resurgent Catholic monarchs. During that long period of relative peace and tolerance it was the home of the three great "peoples of the Book", Christians, Muslims and Jews. The Muslims left behind many symbols of their presence there that contributed to the character of Spain and its people. Among the most spectacular of these gifts is the grand Mesquita-Catedral de Córdoba. The Mosque-Cathedral is a sprawling majestic monument, dating from the fifth century. When the Spanish recaptured the city, they preserved the Mosque and built their Catholic Cathedral within its walls. The Cathedral shrinks in comparison to the giant mosque within which it is contained.

The city was also home to a Jewish quarter that thrived for centuries under the Muslim regime that had a more benign relationship with the Jewish citizens than would exist under the Catholic Monarchs who succeeded them. The Córdoba Synagogue in the Jewish quarter was built in about 1315 and was seized by King Ferdinand in 1492, when the Jews were expelled from Spain. The building survived, although not as a house of worship, and in 1935, the authorities allowed the first Jewish prayer service to be performed there in 443 years. The imprint of the three great religious and cultural traditions were preserved and woven into the Spanish personality. Much later, elements of those characteristics would be assimilated into the Hispano culture who that came to inhabit the Spanish colony of New Mexico. And I found echoes of those qualities in the Hispano people of northern New Mexico I met much later in life.

At the end of my impactful visit to Spain, I returned to the United States on a small Spanish steamer that departed Cadíz and took over a week to reach our *destination in New York. I was met by my parents and there were emotional good-byes to my new friends as we headed off on our separate journeys. It was to be two more years before I moved past that prelude and was first introduced to the New Mexico version of my Spanish preoccupation. I spent much of those two years at Swarthmore College in Pennsylvania, where I first began reading Spanish literature. In one course we read Don Quixote in the original language, good preparation for the next chapter of my life.*

It happened without warning when my impulsive, Quixotic father uprooted the family from Rhode Island and, without apparent plan, brought them to Albuquerque. In anticipation of his dramatic odyssey he had managed to enroll my two brothers in the Putney school for the year, giving him the logistical capacity to carry out his adventure. He abruptly departed his Providence law firm, put my mother and two sisters in the car and headed west without having an identified destination. After a month's journey, they happened upon Albuquerque on a windy March day. After two or three days of contemplation he decided to make the city our new family home. There's more to this exotic tale but it should suffice to conclude by saying that our reduced financial circumstances, and the lure of New Mexico, helped me decide to follow the family west and transfer to the University of New Mexico.

The place overwhelmed me. It was the limitless open space, the vast, visible distances, the mountains, the crisp, dry landscape and the little Hispanic villages and Indian pueblos. The Sandia Mountains towering over the city were reminiscent of the mountains of Madrid I had experienced just two years before. Above all it was the people and the constant sound of spoken Spanish around me every day that once again ignited my youthful romance with things Spanish. It was only later that the link between historic Spain and the unique Hispano homeland of New Mexico would become more obvious to me.

...

As Chris and I were spending more of the daylight hours at our Santa Fe home, I needed an activity to occupy my mind and fill the captive hours. Our long history with the cabin and the intense interest it had generated in the history of our little valley provided a restorative diversion. I could write about it, and I did. I researched New Mexico history and what I could learn of the Santa Rita story. There were few archived sources, but over time I integrated what I found with anecdotal evidence accumulated during our years in Santa Rita. The project was time consuming and ultimately resulted in the publishing of a little book. As Chris's disease progressed, and I needed the escape even more intensely, I began work on a manuscript telling the story of building our straw bale cabin. It took several years of interrupted effort, but Chris was able to be present in early 2016 when a book signing event took place at our local independent bookstore. It was one of her fateful, last public appearances.

By that time, the challenge of caregiving was becoming more difficult, almost unbearable. I was desperate for relief. I turned to the computer for brief periods of escape, letting my imagination run free, sometimes dreaming up outlandish, even sacrilegious, internal monologues that took me away from the grim reality of my life and the unfortunate happenings in the real world around me. Things weren't looking good there either.

Is there a God or not? Let's go on the assumption there is. Here's a scenario. He worked six days to create the Earth many hundreds of millions of years ago. I know it wouldn't take six days with modern technology, but this was a long time ago. He said, "This is just an experiment. I have no idea how it will turn out." He thought he would let it run its course with no interference from him. After all, there was a lot on his plate. The universe is very big, if not infinite, and he could be excused for not focusing on one tiny piece of it.

As we are learning with the help of the Hubble telescope and other scientific marvels, the universe contained stuff and experienced events at even light year distances. I say "contained" because the things we are seeing now with these instruments happened hundreds of millions of years ago, and who knows what may have happened since then that we don't know about yet? And God has responsibility for it all. At least that's my assumption, unless, way, way out there, there could be another God, or who knows, maybe other Gods, like the ancient Greeks believed. Maybe even some women ones. That might be good, because then God, the one we're talking about, could have company, if that's what he wants, unless our God is a woman too.

After some light year travels around his domain, God comes back for a look-see at the Earth and you know he's not happy with what's going on. Who would be? He says, I'm glad this was just an experiment because I don't have to take responsibility for this mess." He went on, "These idiots think I'm running the show, but it's in their hands. Fuck 'em. They're on their own." He took some satisfaction from his original decision to not try this again until he saw how this one turned out. With one last look at the state-of-affairs, he thought bitterly, "It was a God damned mistake." And then, one final shot: "If I didn't know better, this would turn me into an atheist."

...

In early 2016 we were agonizing as a family. Chris could not be left alone. Months earlier, when I tried to be away for shopping or a quick break, Chris would call my cell phone, frantic to know where I was. It became increasingly hard for me to be away. I finally arranged with a local agency to provide a trained, experienced, and kind caregiver to allow me a few hours of relief several days a week. Chris rejected the need for that service, and when the woman arrived, refused to be in the same room with her. We persisted, and Toni would calmly tell Chris, "I'll just be in the computer room if you need me. I won't bother you." Toni was experienced with dementia patients and was unconcerned with Chris's reaction. Her presence allowed me to be away for a few hours at a time, relieved my stress, and permitted me to be out of the house to run errands. Chris never relented, and refused to have any interaction with Toni.

My children and I slowly came to the realization that I could not go on in this way indefinitely, and we began to explore the possibility of placing her in a memory care facility. My Santa Fe son and my out-of-town daughter and son were with me frequently to share the decision making. We researched the local facilities and sought out recommendations. We met with the chief nurse and administrator of the most highly recommended institution. She seemed thoughtful and understanding and assured us the decision we were struggling with was one shared by many families. We were shown the very attractive private rooms and common spaces of the facility and introduced to her staff and some of the patients. It all seemed welcoming, comfortable, and with the informality and ambiance of a resort.

The services and activity options seemed comprehensive and encouraged us to believe this might be the best solution. We reluctantly came to believe it was the right thing for Chris and me. The main concern was our uncertainty about how Chris would respond. She was stubborn, resistant to change, and strong-willed. The chief nurse acknowledged our worries but assured us on several visits, that in her experience, "everyone adjusts" with time and the patients come to welcome the comforting and peaceful routine. She advised us they normally request family members to absent themselves from the patients for several weeks to allow them to familiarize themselves with the new reality, to adjust.

We brought Chris in for an interview during which she sat in stoic silence with little to say while there and when we returned home. We couldn't gauge her likely reaction, and she soon forgot our visit. My looming conclusion was that this option was unavoidable and that the time to act was imminent, but doubts and second thoughts persisted. I detested the idea of losing her and committing her to this fate and spent countless hours and days agonizing over the decision.

In early July this dilemma had been a central part of my life for years but was bringing me to the breaking point. It was the practical and moral issue of how to deal with the slowly diminishing cognitive capacity of my partner. In the early days, it was not an overwhelming issue and required only acceptable accommodation. But as the disease progressed, it began taking away pieces of our shared life that gave meaning and pleasure to the small acts of daily life. Conversations were shallow and plot-less. The exchange of opinions and spontaneous reactions to events, people, and the observed world lost their precision and depth.

Still, the rituals of everyday life persisted and provided some comfort; the morning routine of breakfast preparation, newspaper reading, noisy and mostly ignored television commentary and commercials, provided a façade of normalcy. The repetition of decades old patterns disguised the lack of substance. We were less able to converse about what we were reading or hearing or thinking. She read the morning paper religiously and intensely and then re-read it at noon.

The rest of our normal days were even less stimulating. We relied on familiar activities to give texture and some semblance of meaning to the days. We did chores. We did laundry. We tended the gardens. We might go to The Shed for our favorite enchilada. We went to the post office, a most predictable feature of our days. The short trip filled time that would have weighed heavily. We might take a random drive that at least postponed the tedious time at home with little to do. I had things to do, if I could, but reading or time at the computer trying to turn thoughts into words was perceived by Chris as an escape from my responsibility to help fill the vacuum of her life. She too was bored. We were losing each other, or more accurately, I was losing her.

There were still times when our old intimacy was alive. I told her stories of our life to revive her softening memories. I recited the history of our time together, in Santa Fe, Alaska, Salt Lake, Cleveland, and the thirteen houses we had lived in, and she would smile and say, "Oh, I remember that." She relaxed on the couch and I sat beside her, sometimes holding her hand, and I talked and talked. She listened, sometimes chiming in and remembering some of the good things. I told her I loved her. She smiled and said, "You're a nice boy," and we had some of the feelings for each other we always had.

As time passed, her capacity for the basic processes of living diminished. She started losing things. Life became a morbid game of hide-and-seek. Her brain played tricks on her, making her remember things that never happened and forget things that happened five minutes before. She had trouble operating the shower and the coffee maker. She was not happy where she was, and when I took her to another place, she wasn't happy there. The days got longer and emptier. Bedtime came as a blessed reprieve, allowing us to approach normalcy. She slept well, and after the lights were off, we held hands silently and enjoyed the comforting, warm togetherness until we drifted off. In the morning when I woke first, I saw her relaxed, expressionless face on the pillow. It was the face I had known for all our sixty years. I could imagine she would wake up and be the same woman she had been all those years. Then I would realize it was not to be.

As the journey continued, it became clear that our life was becoming a charade in which she played a role driven by her afflicted brain, and I played the supporting actor, making an effort to provide responses to her initiatives that would give her the greatest comfort or the least pain and confusion. I wondered more often where this was leading, and in her own way, she too began to wonder. Now and then she almost acknowledged what was happening to her and was less resistant to hearing the dreaded word ALZHEIMER'S. Other times she valiantly denied the disease and declared she should be allowed to drive the car again. Then, she sometimes looked me in the eye and said, "One of these days, you're going to dump me beside the road," a heartbreaking accusation to which I would respond, "I would never do that. I love you." Painfully, I knew that one of these days I would indeed leave her figuratively beside the road, with good care to be sure, but nonetheless left behind and forever separated from me.

Wise men and women told me it would not be abandonment. My wife, my partner, no longer exists, I was told. She still cast her shadow on the world, but she was no longer there as the person she was. All that remained was the ravaged container of who she was. I should not feel guilt over removing her from our home and putting her living remains in a place that would be comfortable and calming for her remaining time on Earth. With these assurances I was grudgingly forced to agree it was the right thing to do, and with the inevitable further erosion of her personhood, it would become even more right. That truth didn't reduce the agony of the transition and the foreboding that the passage would be brutal and psychologically destructive to us both. That brought me back to the ultimate dilemma. What was the best way to bridge the gap between yesterday and tomorrow? The transition had to happen. To do nothing would cripple the caregiver while failing to meet the needs of the neurological victim.

Grief was my companion throughout every day. She was gone while she was still there. I had lost her while she was with me. I dreaded our continued life in this prison. I dreaded the separation to come. With most diseases, there is at least the forlorn hope of recovery. With this one, there is no such hope, and without hope, each dawn is a new torture. When I opened my morning eyes, it was to despair and helplessness. But that had been my unfolding fate for longer than I could remember, and I had managed to carry on. Now I began to harbor the guilty hope, the hope that it would all end and that we could be liberated.

It happened. Our daughter, Tina, and our son Harlan were with Chris and me the night before we delivered her to her destiny. All of us except Chris knew that the next morning we would take her to a distant place, right downtown, where she would almost certainly live out her remaining days. We tricked her. We deceived her. With the best of intentions and confident it was the only thing that would be right for her, for me, and the rest of her anguished family, we dropped her off in a good place, but with strangers, and walked away. We could see she was distraught, afraid, and felt abandoned, but we had run out of options, and this option, reached with cool logic, seemed to be the right one.

All the pain of the decision and its execution were followed by more intense grief, almost as if she were not still among the living. There was a sense of finality, separation, a fault line fracture that divided my life between before and after our separation. The evening of the day it happened, Tina and I had dinner in a downtown restaurant, enjoyed a bottle of wine, and listened to the soft, soothing chords of a

Chris 2014

guitar. With a tinge of guilt, we both agreed that much as we grieved, we also felt a profound sense of relief. We were liberated from the prison of our circumstances. It was like the mixed emotions that must be felt by the family of a person who has finally died after a hideous, painful terminal illness. Chris was still there, just around the corner, but she was also gone. As we sat over our last glass of wine, we cried, and we laughed.

A week later and back at the cabin, I sat there in that big beautiful world with a river running through it, looking at the darkening western sky, I began to feel something like renewal, even relief; not enough to quench the sad truth, but still, some help. Tears and loneliness were in the forefront, but despite the intense grief, the moment somehow forced the eye and mind beyond that and allowed me to begin considering what lay ahead.

Back in Santa Fe, the dramatic change could not be ignored. The house was empty and silent, and I was free to come and go as I wished. I hoped against hope that things were well with her in the distant downtown but had little tangible basis for knowing, except for a few cryptic, encouraging messages from the staff at El Castillo Memory Care. "She will be fine when she adjusts. It's challenging at the beginning. I think she likes the staff."

A week later, my son Mason was with me for a few days. We retreated to our Santa Rita sanctuary for a brief stay. We enjoyed a good dinner on a cool August evening. It was just over a month since we had sent Chris away, and it was hard for me to realize that we would never really be together again. I was feeling okay, but everything in those familiar surroundings reminded me of her. When we arrived at the cabin, I noticed her hat on the shelf by the front door and realized that she would never need it again. I put it on the top of the armoire beside an old hat of mine. There were other old hats of hers and her old down vest. Tina, Mason, and I had spent two days removing things of hers from the home place, as if she had left the Earth. Just a month before, Chris and I had been struggling together to approximate what it was like to live as husband and wife. When we slept together, after a hard time getting ready for bed, it almost felt normal. When we turned off the light, I turned to the right and held her right hand with my right hand and we drifted off to sleep. We had gotten up the next morning, and had breakfast, it wasn't much different than it had been a year or two before. The rest of the day was very different, but there were tender moments when we came close to being together as we had been. As I spent the day with Mason, I felt the loss every few minutes. The last few years had been a downward spiral. I certainly hadn't enjoyed those times, but a month after losing her, I missed even the bad times.

The final two months of her cascading ordeal and our agony as helpless spectators was more unbearable than we could have imagined. It started with that bright, sunny July morning when we took her to the euphemistically named memory care facility, expecting it would be her residence for the rest of her time here. It was hoped, almost promised, that she would adjust to the new reality. Everyone adjusts, we were told. It was not to be. She resisted with anger first and then with physical aggression against her captors. Her lifelong strength and tenacity had always served her well, but it became a handicap in the new environment where passivity and compliance were expected. Her mental state declined, and her physical health began to suffer.

Resistance to her circumstances resulted in her being expelled from the memory care facility. They couldn't handle her, they said. She was disturbing the other patients. The staff psychiatrist said she should be moved to a more medically intensive clinic in Albuquerque for aggressive psychiatric care. The staff said that when she had been "stabilized," she would be able to return to El Castillo.

During her brief time in the Albuquerque facility, despite what seemed to be the best efforts of good caregivers, the tumultuous disruption of her life patterns seemed to accentuate her cognitive and physical failings. First there was a fall and more than one emergency room episode. During one of those visits, it was discovered she was suffering with heart arrhythmia. She was then moved by ambulance, a trip of about a hundred yards, to another hospital. That morning, I received a call from an unknown surgeon who advised me that she needed surgery for placement of a pacemaker. If I had had the presence of mind to come to terms with the certainty of her imminent death, I would have rejected the recommendation as an unnecessary insult to her already weakened body, but I didn't have the wisdom or strength to resist. The surgery was performed, and she was returned, again by ambulance, to the intensive care facility. By this time, she had lost her remaining ability to fight the inevitable.

Those brief sentences encapsulate a period of torment for all of us watching this heart-wrenching progression, in isolation, out of her presence, informed and advised only by remote, unfamiliar doctors and caregivers.

The time between delivering her to the Santa Fe memory care facility on July 22 and her death on September 24 was devastating. There was the agony of second thoughts about our decision, anxiety and uncertainty about her care, and a deep sense of loss in her absence. It was the longest and psychologically most painful separation of our shared years. Not only was she out of our life, but we had been advised to not visit her until she had "adjusted" to her new place. That never happened, and our only consolation was that in those few short weeks, she rapidly lost the capacity to be fully aware of her fate.

It was hard to believe that her physical and cognitive condition could have deteriorated so much in the short two months since her Santa Fe confinement. When she began her residency there, she was able to manage reasonably well with the daily routine. She was damaged but still relatively robust, and her will was full-bodied. Early reports confirmed she was not going down without a fight. She swore. She demanded her release and expressed her anger with aggression toward the nurses. All of this was outside my sight and hearing. She was alone and deprived of any support or comfort I could have provided. The requirement of isolation was recommended by those in whose care she had been placed, and I accepted it as reasonable and necessary. Her dramatic decline was evidence that the decision to submit her to care was timely, but the treatment she received, and the course the disease took in the wake of that decision, were heartbreaking to follow from my remote observation point.

The anguish was not mine alone. Our three children were my partners in that journey and shared the tears I shed, suffered their own sense of loss and pain, and had the additional burden of giving me every support and comfort they could. We helped each other, shared memories of happier days, and had the consolation of being together. We grieved during that two-month purgatory and grieved again when she died.

Painful as this account is, it fails to fully capture the brutal details of her last month, for her and me. It was a time of strangely transactional and process centered activity. There was little time to deal with the personal trauma. She had been moved by ambulance from the Santa Fe memory care facility to the Albuquerque behavioral health center, a move initiated by the psychiatrist in the Santa Fe care facility. I had never met or consulted with that doctor and was informed of his recommendations by the chief nurse. What information I received about the subsequent rapidly unfolding events was provided only by cryptic telephone updates and brief visits with a doctor, nurses, and caregivers in the new place. At the end of her stay there, after two ambulance deliveries to and from the emergency rooms and a neighboring hospital, I was advised there was nothing further they could do for her there and she should be discharged. I was in shock and was counseled to explore options for nursing care. I called the Santa Fe facility, which provided nursing care for their patients, but they declined to take her back.

I was at my wits' end, with no sense of how to proceed. Fortunately, the kind social services staffer where she languished offered suggestions of assisted living or nursing care institutions in the Albuquerque area. I immediately visited three of the suggested places. The first two were large, antiseptic, institutional, and lacked the warmth and compassionate human touch I had hoped for. The third place immediately encouraged me to believe it might meet my expectations. It was an attractive, unpretentious house in a quiet residential neighborhood on the edge of the university campus and could accommodate hospice care. Despite its saccharine, euphonious name, "Home Sweet Home," it lived up to its billing and did seem homey. And the women comprising its small staff were sweet, caring, and attentive, several of them Spanish speakers. Further, there were only four or five hospice level patients under their care. My decision was made immediately, and the next afternoon I was there when Chris was delivered to their care by ambulance and settled into this last stop on her life's journey. She was mute and inexpressive but seemed calm and comfortable at last.

In subsequent days, I commuted from Santa Fe, arranged for hospice care, brought a few personal items for her, and had several brief visits as she became adjusted to the home-like surroundings and the warm attention of the staff. My visits were austere and impersonal as she seemed to be unaware or unconcerned with my presence. I was relieved to see changing shifts of older Hispanic women, all of whom seemed attentive, experienced, and totally at ease dealing with the needs of dying patients. Back in Santa Fe, and now aware of her approaching death, I visited and contracted with Rivera Family Funerals to do what would be necessary to deliver her body for cremation when the time came.

During those last days, Chris occasionally recognized me, and warmly, but inarticulately, greeted me, unable to put sentences together. My last time with her was on a Friday. She was weak, looked tiny and fragile, but was sitting in a comfortable chair next to a table in what had been the living room of the house. Soft food had been placed before her that she seemed to be ignoring. She made little effort to talk but held my hand in a viselike grip and looked me in the eye with intensity. I was fully aware for the first time that the welcome end of her torment was near. The staff encouraged me to spoon-feed her the applesauce, but she declined or was unable to eat. I was reminded of trying to spoon-feed a reluctant child in a highchair some decades before. I talked and she listened, looking at me with a small smile. After some time, the woman in charge, who had been solicitous and considerate on all my visits, put her hand on my shoulder and said, "You are welcome to stay as long as you like, but you should know she will be fine when you leave and probably won't know you have left." With her encouragement, I eased my hand out of Chris's grasp, kissed her, and made my painful exit.

The next day, my Santa Fe son, Harlan, came for a visit, and to his surprise, found her more responsive. He had brought his dog, Oatmeal, who was an old friend of Chris's. She seemed confused about him, and Harlan noticed that in addition to her fatal disease, she was further handicapped by not having her glasses that had been a necessity since early childhood. They had gone missing in the tumultuous drama of the past weeks. She responded with some emotion when Oatmeal sat on her foot and nudged her for attention. She smiled, petted him, and seemed to enjoy his touch. She asked for Harlan's wife and children but couldn't remember their names. She acknowledged one of her Hispanic ladies, who spoke almost no English, and said, "She's a nice lady." Harlan told her stories, reminding her of her life, and she responded only by squeezing his hand.

The next day, Sunday, my son Mason arrived in Santa Fe from Seattle. After discussing his mother's condition and concluding that her death was not likely to be immediate, we decided we could spend a night at our cabin, planning to visit her when we would be back the next day. After a restless night, we were up early the next morning, eager to be on our way because there was no cell phone service in our mountain valley. As we made our way up the northern ridge and down the other side into Colorado, we found a signal, and I called to check for messages. I listened to an early morning call from Allison, the hospice nurse, who told me she had been with Chris when she drew her last gentle breath at three in the morning. My heart sank. Allison's message included a few soothing words and encouragement to call her when I could. My next call confirmed that the Rivera Family hearse had already made the trip to pick up her body and had returned with it to their Santa Fe facility. She was in their hands, and we were resigned to know we had said our goodbyes as well as we could.

It was over. My dilemma was resolved by events. I was left with the unanswered questions about how one should best proceed along the path of decision making when there are no good options. There can never be complete certainty that each incremental step is absolutely the right one, but one can't go back to re-examine and second-guess each call. It was a tortured trip that had reached its end. I knew the ultimate outcome could not be avoided, and despite the pain of the transition, we survivors recognized we had to come through that process, accepting the inevitability of the final chapter, and with an undamaged capacity to remember her at her best in the years before the disease took her down.

We were also comforted by knowing that when the end is terrible, it's not terrible when it ends. I had been grieving her loss for years, watching the slow decay of her viability. I can find no better way to express the ambiguity of my feelings than to borrow my daughter's words from a message she wrote a few weeks later.

> *Her illness was so terrible, so difficult, so painful, that in honesty, my grief in the first loss of her was seasoned with a touch of relief. This terrible thing that stole her away from me has ended. The words "relief" and "release" have been often on my lips, as I consoled others who sought to console me. I told them, "It's sad, but it's also a relief." It was so difficult, she was so difficult, and then she left and that was a relief.*

As time passed, relief leaked away, replaced by a dull, heavy, confusing sense of absence, constant reminders of her former presence. But there were things to do. We didn't have the family traditions that would focus our minds and emotions on an early formal funeral ceremony and burial. Chris had years before made her intentions clear. She was cremated and her ashes would be buried in the *camposanto*, the small, rustic cemetery across the river from our cabin. Winter was closing in and the place would be inaccessible until spring. We agreed that a remembrance event would be planned for Christmas time when all her children and grandchildren could be present, and friends could join us for a proper sendoff.

In the meantime, the myriad legal and financial tasks associated with death occupied our minds. A few days after her death, I stopped by Rivera Family Funerals, and without ceremony, accepted a small cardboard box containing her ashes, took it home, and placed it on the floor of my clothes closet. Then there was the obituary to write and the need to report her death to distant friends and family. My children began to help me with the daunting job of sorting clothes and other non-precious belongings suitable for charitable donation. In the spring, the same process would have to be repeated in the cabin.

Staying busy was a blessing. Preparation for the Christmas event was good therapy, and the time flew by. The celebration of Chris was two days after Christmas at the Rio Chama Steakhouse in Santa Fe. Brief comments were made by my children, grandchildren, and me, representing three generations of her family. The most accomplished of those messages was given by her daughter, Tina Smith, then the Lieutenant Governor of Minnesota. As a professional speech giver, she spoke movingly from rough notes. I saved her notes, and some of them are repeated here for what they reveal about Chris and her importance to me and her family. Tina remembered a dinner she and I had years ago when she asked me what was Chris's fundamental quality that held us together through the decades. I told her, "She kept me grounded."

> *When you're grounded, the electricity of life doesn't cause you to short-circuit. You stay connected to what matters. No matter where you are, or whom you are with, you don't forget where you came from. You may even have been a guest at Windsor Castle, a story my mother loved to tell, but you are still who you are. That's what it means to be grounded.*
>
> *Mom was a Midwestern populist. And here I am today, a Minnesota politician, grounded in my mother's populist argument that no one is better than anyone else and everybody deserves to be treated the same. With dignity and respect. Mom could sniff out attitude and entitlement a mile away, and though she was usually polite, she refused to fake it.*
>
> *Mom grounded us in precious friendship. She loved her Alaska League of Women Voters friends who adored her humor and intelligence and organizing capacity. She loved her New Mexico friends, love seasoned liberally with strong opinions and shared personal history.*
>
> *Mom grounded us in the importance of family. She loved us unconditionally. Damn, she loved us fiercely, love expressed with outspoken opinions about what we did and how we did it. Unconditional love did NOT mean unconditional approval. We can still hear her telling us what she thinks. "I don't know why the hell you would do it that way, but whatever!"*
>
> *I spend a lot of time with Minnesota state troopers these days, and one*

of them, Jerry Wells, and I, were philosophizing about love and lifelong relationships with our spouses. Jerry said, "I promised to love her forever, back before I knew how long forever was."

Now that's grounded!

ON TO BETTER TIMES

In the winter of my discontent, blending grief with new beginnings, I occupied my mind and my time with change. I had experienced loss and gained freedom, but freedom for what? I didn't seek a far different life than the one I'd had. It had been a good one, but I was starting without my partner and at a time in life when most people don't think of new beginnings, not to mention new partners. I was in the lower part of my upper eighties, in good health, giving me a chance for as much as another ten years of life. I had learned that the older you are, the more likely it is that you will live beyond the life expectancy you had in your mid-sixties. I could have a meaningful number of years yet to use productively, to waste, or to plan for.

With a history of not being a great planner, having always let unfolding events dictate my future, I saw no reason to deviate from that modus operandi. I would move forward, a day at a time, without caution, ready to take risks and willing to ignore the warnings and advice of people who knew better. Coincidentally, the country was doing the same thing with the recent election of Donald Trump. The country and I were taking a time-out from reality.

I could break with tradition, and, for example, start skiing again at age 86, despite my deteriorating bone density. I could make big decisions, like selling my house and immediately buying another one, contrary to the counsel of hospice advisors. I was scaling back, reducing my overhead, but I was spending more on things that didn't make sense and weren't contributing to my long-term viability. Like many Americans, I was finding it hard to focus on my own issues while being so distracted by the tragedy of our recent election. Sometimes my personal loss seemed to shrink when contrasted with the country's loss.

The long winter after Chris's death was hard, but when spring came, I was able to fill part of the huge hole in my life with a return to my cabin and the people and community there. Being there, doing the chores, keeping up the wood pile, fixing the fence the elk had knocked down, mowing the meadow, all helped me deal with the loss and get on the road to recovery. And Baudelio was there to give me company and support. Our cultural and linguistic differences had stretched out the transition to comfortable intimacy, but by then, we were totally at ease with one another. And we shared our status as widowers. Baudelio's Arlene had suffered with heart disease since she was a child and had died three years earlier. He was an almost constant presence in Santa Rita during the snow-free months, so we had lots of time together. He always had work to do, and at the age of about seventy-five, work was his only play.

His cows were there in the spring and fall, grazing on his and our irrigated meadows. In the summer growing season, they were intended to be up the canyon or on his lower fields so the grass could grow in the meadows for harvest in the fall. Fixing fences and frustrating the wise cows' preference for our inviting grass were a constant chore. The cows always found ways to break the rules and the fences. Tom Sawyer-like, Baudelio "allowed" me to help him with his tasks, and it was a gift to be asked to lend a hand. We had a warm relationship, but he was a quiet man and few words were spoken. I became adept at intuiting his instructions to me, learning to anticipate the tool he needed or when to take my turn digging a fence-post hole.

Over our years together, he had passed on to me much of the history of his family and the ephemeral community of Santa Rita that came into existence in the last years of the nineteenth century and expired as a living community in the mid-twentieth century. The exception was Baudelio's family, who continued to live and work there part-time well into the new century. He also contributed to my knowledge of the nearby villages and the surrounding communities of the southern San Luis Valley of Colorado and New Mexico. Chris Garcia became another of my friends and an informant on the place and its people. Chris had purchased and was slowly restoring the old neighboring house that had been the home of his grandparents when he was a boy.

Baudelio and I were now the solitary *viejos*, the old ones, in Santa Rita. At the end of his work day, we might enjoy a beer on my porch or his, just down the road, and occasionally he would share my dinner and spend the night at my cabin rather than make the forty-five minute commute over the northern ridge to his other house and farm in Mogote. These words may begin to explain our relationship and how it helped to mitigate my loss.

¿Quantos animales tienes? How many animals do you have? The number of animals a man owns has been a measure of his wealth and achievement and a testament to the continuity of life in these parts for ages. At the northern edge of the Hispano homeland, along a little noticed valley on the edge of a river that's big in the spring and modest in the summer, the last survivor continues his lifelong pattern of bringing the mother cows and their calves over the ridge from Colorado to New Mexico. It's the end of April, and Baudelio had to wait a week in order to get the inspector's approval before moving the cattle

across the state line. He's engaged in interstate commerce! One mother cow beat the deadline and brought her new baby and last year's steer over the hill early, following the trail she knew by heart and not waiting for the farmer's permission.

This little fragment of a four-century-long migration pattern began when Baudelio's great-grandparents moved up the little Rio de Los Pinos, from who knows where in the late 1800s, probably with a few cattle and maybe some sheep, to a place they had had their eye on for a few years. They were Spanish, or thought they were. They couldn't tell you much about their heritage more than two or three generations back, but their gene pool included lines going back to the people who came to Mexico in the sixteenth century from Spain. Along the path of their journey north, these people had domesticated their line by adding the blood of Mexican Indians and probably New Mexico Indians they met along the road.

When they found their way to this destination, they were still Católicos,

The cows rule

whatever that meant, and they practiced their faith as well as they could with little help from the occasional priest and the remote hierarchy of the church in Santa Fe. Mostly, they were too busy surviving to give great attention to the minutiae of their denomination, but they were people of faith, and their religious commitment was a central part of their daily life.

I look out at a landscape that is a testament to their vision and their strength. There are meadows on both sides of the rushing river, fed by the slowly melting snow in the high country of a Colorado wilderness fifteen or twenty miles upstream. When the pioneers came to the valley, they began to tame the uneven, more-or-less flat land in the riparian plain that could be put under irrigation, using their horses and oxen and primitive tools to get the job done. The biggest task was creating the acequias that delivered the water from the stream to the irrigated meadows. The families probably lived here seasonally for a time, building log or jacál structures where the women could provide a precarious home place for their husbands and children as they tried to carve out a more permanent place for themselves.

As I sit on the porch of my comfortable straw bale cabin, with electricity, a good wood stove to deal with an early May snowstorm, and good well water to do the dishes, I think about what it would have been like in the 1890s without these amenities, and it leaves me with a sense of awe for what these people accomplished not that long ago.

They came here about 120 years ago and started a community they called Santa Rita that persisted into the twentieth century. The community increased to maybe fifteen or twenty families in the 1920s, and then quickly dwindled down to one extended Garcia family in the 1950s, then to one persistent family in the 1960s, and now one man, Baudelio Garcia, who still maintains the acequias and tends the irrigated meadows I look out at in 2017. This is the trailing edge of a 125-year time capsule containing this valley and its sample of the centuries-long journey of the Hispano people. When Baudelio comes over the ridge from Colorado tomorrow, I will welcome him and ask, "¿Quantos animales tiene?"

...

At the beginning of the seventeenth century, Miguel de Cervantes had just created his mythic masterpiece, perhaps the world's first novel. It described the sometimes sad, sometimes delusional but always heroic adventures of the sorrowful knight, Don Quixote and his loyal squire and friend, Sancho Panza. *Don Quixote* heralded the end of the age of chivalry and the gradual decline of the Spanish Empire. The times were changing and the courageous knight and his sidekick were finding it impossible to change with the times.

The time in history when the great book was written coincided with the arrival here of the ancestors of those who would become known as the Hispano people of New Mexico. The New Mexico settlers were launching an endeavor that proceeded relatively uninterrupted for two hundred and fifty years, until the American conquest in 1846. The people of that long era were described by Fray Angélico Chavez, in his much honored *My Penitente Land.* Chavez concluded that, as with Quixote and Panza at the beginning of the seventeenth century, the Hispano people of the middle of the nineteenth century were hard pressed to cope with the changes brought on by the American invasion. It should be noted that Chavez didn't call the people Hispanos. He insisted they should be called *españoles.* Most historians question his characterization of those people as racially or ethnically pure *españoles.* Some of the settlers who came north from Mexico, were only one generation removed from the Iberian Peninsula. Others shared the blood blend of Mexican Indians.

Another genetic and cultural element in the New Mexico mix was provided by the people who have come to be called Cripto-Jews. With the expulsion of Jews from Spain in 1492, some of them accepted forced conversion to the Catholic faith as the only means to remain in Spain. They were called *conversos.* Some of these people or their descendants came to Mexico and then New Mexico, often having lost all awareness of their Jewish heritage but unconsciously retaining cultural artifacts of their historic past; Jewish toys, Friday night candles. In recent times many New Mexicans have been made aware of their ancient religious connection and have proudly proclaimed their status as Crypto Jews. Fray Angelico Chavez was one of them, having found that two of his ancestors were *conversos.*

Yet another contributor to the New Mexico blend are the *genízaros.* These New Mexicans trace their roots to people, sometimes detribalized Indians, who were of mixed Spanish and Indian blood. This genetic blend is often found in people who were the victims of both Spanish and Indian raids against each other. The captured people, often women and children, became articles of trade and were sometimes sold and kept as virtual slaves by their captors. Over time they sometimes came to be accepted as full members of their host families. These genetic and cultural streams combined to form what we call the Hispano people. Angelico Chavez saw himself as one of these Hispano people. He wrote about them and clearly loved them passionately. Perhaps he aspired to be called the Cervantes of the Hispano people, celebrating their history and honoring their place in the historical continuum of a culture he viewed as stretching back over the centuries to its ancient Castilian roots.

It is telling that Chavez was a romantic Franciscan friar and brought that perspective to his role as observer, admirer and chronicler of his New Mexican *españoles.* He was fortunate that the forward to the 1993 edition of his book was written by Thomas J. Steele, S.J., a skeptical, intellectual scholar and Jesuit priest. Fr. Steele brought a more hard-nosed and evidence driven analysis than did Chavez. He admired and applauded Chavez but was skeptical about some of the more exuberant passages in his book, saying it "resembles its author: cantankerous, waspish, opinionated, outrageous, entertaining, charming, delightful, knowledgeable, intuitive, intelligent...." In any event, Chavez elegantly described much of what we recognize and admire in the people some of us call Hispanos.

Despite the disruption caused by the American acquisition of New Mexico and the inevitable social, cultural and economic transformation that occurred, there are still strong surviving elements of the old ways and traditional qualities we find in the people we meet in La Jara, San Antonio, Ortiz, Capulín, Colorado, and Santa Rita, Los Pinos, Ojo Caliente and other New Mexico communities. As in much of the rest of the country during the last hundred years or more, many rural New Mexicans have been drawn out of their small towns and villages and have migrated to the cities and urban centers. Notwithstanding that drastic change, the villages and remnant rural populations left behind, persist and sustain the traditions and, importantly, the Spanish language of the people who remain.

Given the fanciful excesses of Fray Angélico Chavez's story, he still captured the historic characteristics of his *penitente* Hispanos and the distinctive world in which they lived. Fr. Steele endorsed "his ruminations about the economic foundation of Hispanic New Mexico before the land losses of the nineteenth and twentieth centuries pulled the Hispanics out of their homes in the mountain valleys, away from the extended family values that can survive in a village setting but not in the urban world of wage-work, consumerism, democratization and individualism." Even with those losses, the villages today sustain many of their ancient qualities.

In rural northern New Mexico and southern Colorado, Chavez observed and celebrated the "upland herdsmen, ...the *anima hispanica,* the Spanish soul... the tangible Castilian landscape" that he saw transported from ancient Castile and replicated in New Mexico. He celebrated the ambiance of the place, its "sharp sunlight on stark terrain...sad and severe but never morbid" and linked it with the landscape of Don Quixote's La Mancha. As in ancient Palestine and medieval Castile, he saw that the land of the northern Hispano Homeland was "made for erect shepherds, not for stooping peasants" and concluded that "the prevailing way of life was therefore *pastoral*, not agricultural...which sets the shepherd or stockman distinctly apart from the farmer...."

This description, exaggerated as it may be, fits the history and traditions of the people of this region and their landscape. Sadly, the economic and societal changes have brought some of these strong, independent people out of the villages and the pastoral highlands into the cities, towns and suburbs and have diminished and damaged many them and made them especially vulnerable to the ills of substance abuse, poverty, unemployment, obesity and the other tragic expressions of cultural decay and subjected them to the common American maladies. Those outcomes were not inevitable. Many more Hispanos have successfully made the transition and have found their place as leaders in the new environment, while retaining what they value from their root culture.

Even in the twenty first century, the old patterns of life vigorously survive in the rural neighborhoods like Santa Rita, San Miguel, Mogote and the other villages of the north. In the spring when the herdsmen take their stock to the mountains and in the fall when they bring them down for the winter, the Hispano families gather on horseback with their shepherd dogs to manage the cattle and sheep in the same way they have for generations. Fray Angélico would probably see these contemporary riders as "examples of the nearly universal man-on-horseback archetype so especially powerful in the Spanish world". These modern ranchers and herdsmen would be mystified by such grand metaphorical elevation of their ordinary seasonal routine. Yes, they have been urbanized to a degree, and have moved on to contemporary American lifestyles, but they proudly maintain their traditions, treasure their strong, extended family bonds and, sometimes, retain their unique version of the Spanish language.

...

It had been a stormy late April stay at the cabin with light snow falling most of one day. The following morning there were a few inches on the ground. I drove down the three-mile forest service road to San Miguel to my friend Peter Shoenfeld's cabin and barn where I had left my trailer and riding mower for the winter. I had hoped to bring the mower back to Santa Rita for the summer. The road down was cushioned by the new snow and I made first tracks. Peter wasn't there and his gate was locked, so in a way it was a wasted trip, but I was happy for the excuse to be the only one out and about.

It also gave me a chance to take a picture of the little stone church in San Miguel. It is a lovely structure, like many hundreds of others all over New Mexico, signaling the presence of Hispano villages that have often shriveled close to oblivion as their people have moved on to other ways of life. San Miguel is one of those villages. There are small houses scattered over the valley, but they are occupied only occasionally and seasonally. At this writing, there is only one surviving full-time resident in San Miguel. Despite that, the fields are still irrigated, cattle still graze, and there are many dispersed former residents and their progeny who still consider this to be their *patria chica*, their home place. Sons and grandsons, living in the larger, surrounding communities, irrigate the meadows, cut and bale the hay, and manage the livestock. The families who trace their origins to San Miguel often gather for giant annual reunions, sometimes over a hundred people, from nearby and distant places. They arrange for a priest to be there to conduct a Mass in the village church. This church, like many others, has long since been deconsecrated, but it still stands, is cared for and maintained as an honored community treasure. Churches like this one are restored and repaired and preserved by the diaspora of people who came from the place. These churches are revered for their religious significance, but perhaps as important, because they are symbols of community. And they are beautiful.

Symbol of community

When I returned from my ride, the bird feeders were going crazy. There were even about twenty ravens hanging around waiting for seeds to be scattered, and there must have been twenty finches and other little birds on the thistle feeder. The stellar jays and magpies were working on the seed cake. The snow continued gently but persistently. The temperature was an un-spring-like 17 degrees at breakfast time when I had bacon and blue corn johnnycakes. It was only in the mid-twenties through the day.

I did a thorough spring cleaning of the whole house and found a desiccated mouse behind a yoga mat in the middle bedroom. No other major finds. I had brought up my Alaska parka the previous Christmas and wore it for a comfortable walk after lunch to admire the river and the new stream retention structures we had installed in the fall. After a good dinner in my sparkling clean house, I looked out the front door and saw the biggest elk herd I had ever seen in my forty years in the valley. They were right in front of me, and as I watched, more came down from the trees on the other side of the river. They were bunched up and hard to count, but there must have been thirty of them. I couldn't see any antlers, so it may have been too early, or perhaps they were mostly cows and yearlings. I didn't see any new calves. What a sight! They looked my way occasionally, and ultimately, on a signal I couldn't detect, they all took flight and raced up the slope into the trees. I was fortunate to be there at a special time. At 7:30, it was a gray dusk, and at 8:00, it was approaching pitch dark.

I remember playing solitaire with a pack of cards that said "Chris" on the cover, in her hand; cards that were over the hill but declared her former presence.

Welcome Guests

I was slowly erasing evidence of her existence there, but the bulletin board was frozen in time, the photo collection not having been upgraded since she last did it. How could we remove the photos she posted, and what could we replace them with? There were other reminders of her at every turn, indoors and out. I was doing well, thinking of her often, sometimes uttering a forlorn, "Oh Chris!" triggered by a poignant memory, but still looking forward with pleasure to what came next.

I remember often thinking how fortunate I was to be able to do whatever I wanted, with no significant physical limitations. How long that would last nobody could know, and that was fine with me. I was comfortable and ready to continue as long as that was the way it was. And if I were to fall and couldn't get up, I was okay with that too. It had all been good, still was, and when it was over, that would be okay too.

I checked the outside temperature, and finding it was down to 20 degrees, I went out to bring in the hummingbird feeder. That morning the feeder had been almost solid ice, but a hummingbird was trying to feed, so I had waited before bringing it in. It was always satisfying at the end of a cold day to be in a warm, cozy house that I built, and to be there on a hard winter night at the end of April was even more satisfying. I went to sleep with visions of enjoying a red chile cheese enchilada with onions at the Mesa Vista Café on the way home to cap off a good round trip.

My son Harlan and I spent one June weekend in Santa Rita with three fourteen-year-old boys—my grandson Jasper and his friends, Gabe and Luke. The boys camped out for two nights at an upstream campground owned by the Salopek family, well-to-do pecan farmers from Las Cruces in southern New Mexico. The boys were surprised on the second morning by one of their even more surprised hosts, a big intimidating guy with a brash manner. He pulled into their camp and challenged the boys, teasingly, he thought, frighteningly they thought, asking them who the hell gave them permission to trespass. He later visited with Harlan and me, assuring us he was happy to have them. He was with his "girlfriend," later identified as his fiancée, and her children. She and her children were Hispanos from Tierra Amarilla. It was a slightly jarring cross-cultural juxtaposition—a relationship that might cause him to be described as the black sheep of the family back home, in the more conservative southern New Mexico community.

By midmorning there were big cotton ball clouds drifting across an indigo sky. Harlan and the kids were up the valley to collect their camp and clean up the place. Over their three-day visit, the boys had used up more than a tank of gas on their innumerable round trips on the ATV to their camp and anywhere else they could go on the four-wheeler. The river was still a torrent, and its sound was with us full-time. A year before, Chris and I had finished our decades of joint visits there, and she was more comfortable in the security of her Santa Fe home.

With the three boys, one father, and one grandfather together, I thought of the three very different perspectives we would have on the days and years ahead. The young ones were able to live in the idyllic present. They rode three-deep on the ATV designed for one rider. They chattered constantly, conversations exclusively for the three of them, leaving the father and me on the outside. For that day, at least, they had no concern for the future.

The father's focus was divided between now and later. His immediate priority was caring for the boys and sharing their enjoyment of the moment, but he carried with him the challenges of life that couldn't be put on hold. For him, the present and the future were starkly overlapping; there to be managed and accommodated as well as possible. For the grandfather, the occasion involved a different kind of looking back, looking forward, and absorption with the here and now.

While thinking those thoughts, I was sitting on the sunny east side of my cabin. Close by my chair was a sizable boulder, glinting with mica stars and displaying on its face a bronze plaque recording the spare vital statistics of Christine Mason Flint's life. Across the roaring river, barely visible through the trees, was the little fenced cemetery, the destination later that summer of the marker and her ashes.

Next to my chair was a tiny garden of wild iris, put there who knows when by the forces of nature. To my left, just past the tailgate of my truck, was the thistle feeder on the side of the shed, swarming with finches and pine siskins. Looking out at those things, seeing and hearing all that was spread out before me, I felt good about where I was on this perpetual but constantly changing planet. The past had been good to me, and for most of her journey, for Chris too. Despite the pain, I was okay with the past, the present, and whatever the future might hold.

...

At about this time, there was another unanticipated turn in my road. Some years earlier, Chris had found an old friend in Santa Fe, a woman she had been close to when they were both students at Indiana University. They rediscovered each other after we returned in retirement, and we had enjoyed time together with her and her husband for several years. Close to the time of Chris's death, the friend and her husband moved to California. Sometime later, after learning about Chris, she emailed me and a woman friend of hers in Santa Fe, suggesting that we might enjoy spending some time together. Chris had been gone for only about nine months, and I was somewhat reluctant to open that door, but encouraged by the message, I called Lynn and we had a blind date lunch. It was my first such experience in over sixty years, and I think it was the first real date Lynn had had since losing her husband some ten years before.

We were both soon at ease in that unfamiliar setting and found common ground. It was late June of 2017, and like many people, we were riveted by the madness of our new president. We discovered a mutual concern for where we were going as a country. The common ground of our political leanings was an easy and reassuring lubricant. Our lives had been very different, and we were interested in and curious about our divergent paths. I was a recovering lawyer and long retired corporate executive. She had a lifelong connection with journalism, having started work as a crime reporter for the Philadelphia *Bulletin* after college. Soon after that, she married a fellow journalist at the *Bulletin* who went on to a stellar career, culminating with years as editorial page editor for the *Los Angeles Times*.

Dare I say she was more of a city girl from Philadelphia, and I, despite years in Cleveland, San Francisco, and Salt Lake, felt more like a country guy from out

Lynn Day 2020

west. We could argue about that. We shared a similar sense of humor. At least she laughed at my jokes. We didn't learn all of that during our first lunch at the Santacafé, but in subsequent lunches and dinners, we became more of an item, if that's not too dated a turn of phrase. We enjoyed and looked forward to our time together. We didn't have many friends in common. As a widow of ten years with no consistent male companion, she had a wide circle of friends, mostly couples, whom she spent time with and often entertained. I was quickly included in her active social life. My circle was much smaller and had been growing even smaller with the passing years, and the passing of friends, for that matter.

Lynn Day had spent her early years in Paoli, a mainline suburb of Philadelphia. After graduating from Penn State, she returned to Philadelphia, teamed up with two other women, and rented a $65-a-month "dump" apartment in the city. She was the only woman on the night shift at the newspaper and sometimes brought friends and colleagues home for drinks and conversation in the middle of the night, disturbing her roommates who had normal daytime jobs.

Lynn was sometimes a crime reporter and had made a name for herself with a bylined article about a woman accused of murdering her husband. Lynn was able to report that the wife had recently been loaned a copy of *Anatomy of a Murder*, evidence that may or may not have helped the jury reach a verdict of guilty. Lynn's father was not pleased that his daughter was involved in such shady matters.

My love affair with the cabin and the relationships it produced continued to be a vital part of my life, now often including Lynn. On one of our stays, we visited with Chris Garcia. He had acquired the lovely but decrepit old Garcia house next to ours that had been his grandparents' home when he was a child. The house had been unoccupied for decades, was in bad repair, and Chris was in the long, slow process of lovingly restoring it to its original condition.

He stopped at my cabin to enjoy a cold glass of our wonderful water on my porch. Chris is one of the top lawyers in the statewide legal aid office headquartered in Albuquerque. That institution provides legal assistance in civil matters for people of limited means who are otherwise without legal representation and at the mercy of sometimes unscrupulous adversaries.

Budgetary stress threatened the potential layoff of nineteen lawyers in his office, causing chaos for the office and its clients. Most of the lawyers were looking for other employment because of the threat. The firm had lost its one lawyer in Silver City who was tasked with trying to meet the needs of poor people in the vast southwest region of the state. They had also lost their one attorney in Las Vegas, New Mexico, and were down to one or two in Santa Fe. The staff in Albuquerque was burdened with the heartbreaking chore of turning away clients who were losing their mobile homes to unethical vendors or were tenants dealing with unscrupulous landlords. The result was that thousands of New Mexicans, most of them Hispano people of modest means, were being put in serious jeopardy because of lack of representation. It's sad to be reminded that these people are unable to defend themselves while those of us who have the means can protect ourselves against such threats. It is scandalous that the most vulnerable are deprived of the most basic protection. Remnants of the state's historic Anglo-Hispano divide still exist.

Chris and I had been friends for years and had earned each other's trust. We had visited often, exchanged emails, and he had contributed to work on my writing with suggestions, insights, and critiques. There continues to be deep-seated suspicion and resentment in the Hispano community because of the historic abuses they suffered at the hands of Anglos. Chris and I have been able to erase that traditional boundary of distrust on a personal level, and that has allowed me to learn more about how Chris, his family, and friends view the still sensitive dividing line between us and them. Many Hispanic writers have explored these issues, but I am privileged to learn about the Hispano experience firsthand.

In the early twentieth century, the little village of Santa Rita where Chris Garcia's family took root was a microcosm of the larger Hispano community of New Mexico. The experience of the Hispano people was genuinely unique. For two and a half centuries, they had lived in a homogeneous community, undiluted by any significant European admixture until the Americans came in 1846. Suddenly they became part of a new country within which they were treated as a minority group in their ancient homeland. The Americans replaced their hegemony and held disparaging opinions of the "Mexicans" they had defeated in the Mexican War. Many of the natives, as they were sometimes called, still lived in their largely Hispano communities, but their villages became isolated islands in an Anglo sea. That was true in Santa Rita.

The people generally embraced their American citizenship, but there were big changes coming. They still spoke Spanish in the home but were introduced to English in school. They borrowed money. They earned dollars and traded in Anglo stores. They mortgaged their properties to Anglo lenders. The subsistence farm and ranch land in Santa Rita had little financial value, and even small debts or property tax obligations put pressure on people just getting acquainted with the cash economy. As time passed, they began to move out of the valley for jobs, for military service, or for the perceived benefits of the new society. They also began to sell their homesteads to Anglo outsiders who found new values in these properties in the high country wilderness. In time, only the Antonio and Juanita Garcia family lived full time in the valley, the last survivors of the homesteader families.

In the larger communities of the San Luis Valley, the arrival of the Americans had changed the social and political status of the Hispanos. Some would say that they became citizens and second-class citizens at the same time. Anglos soon had the upper hand, and discrimination was rampant. Richard Nostrand, in his book, *The Hispano Homeland*, said most of the newly arrived Americans believed "that they represented a superior civilization and, with contempt, they described

New Mexicans as indolent, degenerate, undependable, dishonest, impoverished, and addicted to gambling and other vices." The disrespect and discrimination suffered by the original New Mexicans gave rise to one of the country's first civil rights organizations. It was organized in Antonito in 1900 with the grand name, *La Sociedad Protección Mutuo de Trabajadores Unidos*, roughly translated as The Mutual Protection Society of United Workers, better known as SPMDTU. It was created to protect land rights, language, and culture, and to prevent wage discrimination. Santa Rita homesteaders were among its members.

In the Hispano world, the vast land that became the national forests had been perceived, under Spanish and Mexican law and usage, as the *ejido,* commons, available to all for timber harvesting, firewood gathering, grazing, hunting, and fishing. That changed under American law and practice. The new owners of property previously owned by the locals frequently had a more exclusive sense of ownership, and the National Forest land that had been communally shared in the past was now off limits or required costly permits. The practices of exclusion were resented by those who still had a strong connection to the land that had comprised their homeland, their *patria chica.*

The children of the valley, like Chris Garcia, grew up knowing every nook and cranny of the Rio de Los Pinos canyon. They had fished and hunted in all the side canyons and high meadows. What had been their open park and wilderness was now less available. That, and the enduring vestiges of ancient prejudice, must have weighed heavily on the new generations of Garcias and their cohorts. I'm always conscious of that history when I'm with my neighbors in Santa Rita or visiting with the cast of players at the Mesa Vista Café, and I'm grateful that the broad historic injustice doesn't prevent the possibility of reconciliation and friendship.

...

One summer weekend, I drove up through the San Luis Valley to Alamosa, Colorado for a stop at the place where I bought my new ATV, but they were closed. The drive took me past the tiny village of Manassa, the hometown of Jack Dempsey, the famous boxer known as the Manassa Mauler. The trip wasn't a total waste as it gave me another chance to quietly contemplate the city of Alamosa. It's the closest city, large enough to serve as our local shopping venue, about an hour and a half drive from Santa Rita. It is surrounded by the high mountains and stands at about 7,800 feet elevation. Despite that altitude, it is close to the low point in the giant San Luis Valley. Because of its location and elevation, winter temperatures can be as low as minus 30 degrees at night and still be mild in the daytime, with circadian temperature swings of forty degrees.

An early civil rights organisation - Antonito

Alamosa is not a tourist destination. It's a working place, a town where hardworking people are trying to find their way up the American economic ladder. The city looks like many medium sized towns in middle America. There is a long strip commercial district, stretching east to west. A train track divides the city, passing through the city center with its older commercial buildings, shops, bars and restaurants. The Rio Grande flows by the east side of town on its way south. It struck me that almost all the town's street names are Spanish, while the active life of the community has a distinctly Anglo character. There is little sign of the early Hispanic footprint, just a few Mexican restaurants. The old New Mexico Hispanos were the first Europeans to arrive, but today the population mix is much more diverse, even among the Hispanics. Alamosa came into being shortly after the first European settlement in what is now Colorado, in about 1852. The oldest families trace their roots back to the Hispano homeland in New Mexico, but there are a lot of the new Hispanics, more recently arrived from Mexico and other

Central American countries. These newer arrivals were often refugees escaping economic and criminal stress in their home countries. The population of the town and surrounding agricultural community also includes Mormons who came early, after the Civil War, and the community attracted a grand mix of other eastern Anglo Americans and nineteenth-century immigrants from Europe.

The flat valley supports a substantial agricultural economy, producing mostly alfalfa now, along with a few potatoes, and a sprinkling of wheat, oats, and even hops for the Coors breweries. There is very little precipitation in the valley, and the crops are dependent on the runoff from snow in the surrounding mountains, delivered through an extensive network of irrigation ditches taking water from the Rio Grande and its tributaries. Alamosa is a regional marketing center serving the widely dispersed rural and small community population.

As I drove north in the morning, I passed dozens of flatbed trucks loaded with hay bales headed south, most likely to Texas. Most of the other vehicles on the road were pickups with the windows down even on a hot summer day. There were big new pickup trucks with prosperous looking farmers, and there were smaller, older trucks with people who may be doing the service and support jobs that keep the wheels turning. There were even a few horses and buggies, driven by Amish citizens who have recently joined the community. The town hosts Adams State College, part of the Colorado State system, plus a branch of Trinidad Community College.

I headed back south toward Antonito, west on the Chama highway, then south from Mogote toward our place on the other side of the high ridge in New Mexico. I didn't see Baudelio's truck at his house in Mogote, but his son-in-law, Frenchie, waved me down to tell me that he and Baudelio had repaired my trailer that had broken down on a previous trip to Alamosa. Frenchie is really Pascal Jean Antoine, born outside Nancy, France, but as with any French immigrant in the wild American west, he was destined to be called Frenchie. I hooked up the trailer and made my noisy way over the ridge.

Baudelio was sitting on the porch of his Santa Rita cabin when I pulled in. A lead cow, followed by other cows and calves, was coming down the road from up above, ready to join her group with the rest of the herd in Baudelio's lower meadow. He told me he had pushed them all up the canyon every day of the last four, trying to keep them out of our hay fields, but that same head cow kept bringing them back down. I had seen this same calm, docile looking cow confidently leading her brigade down the road more than once. Baudelio said, "I'm going to have to get rid of that darned cow." Being a leader is not always a good thing. It can mean becoming hamburger before your time.

Baudelio looked old and tired, showing all his seventy-five years. He had been fixing fences for the past three days, trying to stay ahead of the cattle who admired our tempting hay fields. The new bull had broken through the fence down by the corral twice, in an excess of testosterone and an overwhelming desire for togetherness with his harem. It was hard work for Baudelio, even with occasional help from Frenchie, and the many decades of hard work were taking their toll.

He was the last survivor of this way of life in our small part of the San Luis Valley. There are still some young ones and a few old ones from his stock who follow the old ways in the larger valley below, but it's a tough life and many of the people are only doing it part-time. I wondered how long he would be able to keep it up. He had struggled with diabetes for a long time, and his daughter and son-in-law were worried about him, ready for him to take it easier, but they didn't want to put too much pressure on him. They knew this way of life was in his blood, and to bring it to a complete stop might take him to the threshold of death. I had had a much easier life, and despite my age, knew I had a good chance of seeing him out. I was often reminded that when he left, our little valley would be a far different place. Nobody looked forward to that day.

Time takes its toll

In late July it was impossible for me to forget that it had been a year since we sent Chris to El Castillo. I thought of the confident administrator who had convinced us that "everyone adjusts." I remembered Tina, Harlan, and I making our first exploratory visit and being introduced to five or six of the residents. Some were charming, friendly, and accessible, but with little acknowledgment or awareness of their former lives. Others were passive, mute, and seemingly unaware even of their present state. All was quiet, subdued, and under control.

Our patient was another story. Chris had been a growing challenge. She was deeply impaired with memory loss, increased confusion, fear that required the close, continued presence of a caregiver, decreasing physical capacity that carried a risk of falling, and the distinctive shuffling gait of Alzheimer's patients. On the other hand, she could get herself up in the morning with supervision, enjoy her modest traditional breakfast, read the paper—perhaps more than once—watch TV, take her shower with guidance, get herself dressed, and perhaps, with help, adjust the thermostat to a comfort level.

A lifetime of practice let her participate in some of the routines of housekeeping. She no longer contributed to the process of meal preparation, although she would protest that she did most of the cooking. We had maid service, so neither she nor I did any serious house cleaning. She liked to do laundry, although I did almost all of it by then. She liked to do ironing, and to my never-ending sadness, ironed two of my shirts on the afternoon before we subjected her to El Castillo.

It was her level of consciousness that gave us the most agonizing challenge in the last months and weeks together. She could talk with us and we could talk to her. She knew who we were and still had some sense of self. She loved me and loved us, her family. She was fighting her disease in a last-ditch battle, never ready to give up. Incapacitated as she so clearly was, she was still a person and not oblivious and acquiescent, like the more incommunicative patients at El Castillo, and certainly not like the ones who were totally off the field of play, permanently beyond the possibility of mental pain and anguish over their state.

But Chris, even in her diminished state, was still Chris, and she was not the person they and we hoped she would be. When we, Tina, Harlan, and I, delivered her to her fate on that July date, she did not go quietly into the oblivion the other patients accepted; the passive, accepting, defeated dementia victims who had lost the need and the capacity to resist. She met the situation with the attitude of a prisoner who was unjustly being deprived of her liberty and illegally separated from her home and family. She did not accept her fate. She rejected the idea of her incarceration. She desperately wanted and expected to be rescued from her unjust confinement. We were not aware of how desperately she was fighting her situation. We were hoping against hope that her adjustment would be as projected by the staff and that she would find peace and comfort.

I learned how false that hope was two or three days later when she managed to outwit a savvy nurse and gain control of her telephone. My damaged but resilient wife used the stolen phone, remembered our home phone number and reached me with a heartbreaking plea for help. She said, "Harlan, you've got to get me out of here. They won't let me go. I want to come home." Can anyone imagine how I felt and how horrible it was to hear that plea from the woman I loved and had lived with for all those years?

The only thing I could think to do was to lie to her, knowing that my lie would be forgotten. I said, "I can't do it today, but I will come for you tomorrow." She said, "Promise?" and I said, "I promise." I said, "I love you," and she said, "I love you too," and then with a break in her voice, she said, "Bye...Bye." It was the most wrenching moment of my life and still is whenever I allow myself to think about it. Those were the last words she spoke to me while she still fully comprehended who we were. The next few brief times we were together, she was crossing that boundary, but not beyond the capacity for pain. The words are still with me. "Bye...Bye."

When that exchange comes back to haunt me, I try to push it aside and heed the advice of those who urge survivors to resist the pull of guilt. I don't often allow myself to relive the symptoms of self-blame, but looking back on that awful anniversary, one year after we had "dumped" her, it was impossible to put aside the lingering memory of that painful last conversation.

...

On a warm summer day, my children, Tina, Harlan, and Mason, their spouses, most of my grandchildren, and I gathered in Santa Rita to bury Chris's ashes in the little cemetery on the hillside across the river. The only clearly identified grave in the *camposanto* was that of Francisco Archuleta, who died at the young age of thirty-one in October of 1931. It was marked by a simple wooden cross, a copy of the one we had seen there when we first visited the grave site in 1977 or 1978. The original was stolen sometime after that, but I had taken a photo of it that displayed the bare facts of his death, and I later made and installed the reproduction.

Chris's ashes were in a simple plastic bag provided by the mortuary last year, and we all debated what would be an appropriate container for burial. Someone reminded us of her love for the birds we enjoyed so much. It was son Harlan who spotted the old birdhouse fastened to a fencepost at the edge of the meadow, and we agreed that it would be the best possible coffin. It was detached, brought up, opened to remove the last old bird nest, and to our great satisfaction, we were able to stuff the bag of ashes into its cavity.

After lunch we trooped across the old bridge and up the hill to the *camposanto*. We took turns digging a small grave, large enough and deep enough to contain the birdhouse. We shared the simple task of covering the grave, expressing our thoughts and memories, and stamping down the loose dirt. The small but heavy boulder, sparkling with mica, had been carried across the river on our hearse, the ATV, and was tenderly placed at the head of the little grave.

The only additional ceremony was the reading of the few words shown below and read by me, until, overcome by the emotion produced by hearing my own words, I turned to Tina to complete the task. We left Chris there, walked back across the river, and returned to the cabin in good spirits and with a few tears.

This marker is a small reminder of a remarkable life. We don't need this modest monument to remember her, but it will touch us in later years and remind us of the time we overlapped with her. Those memories will be most distinct for me while I'm here and for those of you who hang around for varying parts of the twenty-first century. Despite her life being so remarkable for us, the circle of people who will recall her will be small. That's fine and as it should be. Most of us who have good and successful lives don't leave a lasting imprint on history. This marker will be here for perhaps a century or two or three and may intrigue people who will not know her or us. Chris will be forgotten, and Donald Trump will live on in history. Better to be Chris and forgotten by a few than Trump and remembered by millions. Individual lives are transient, but life is more-or-less eternal. This place demonstrates that truth better than most; the cycles of life, measured in seasons, years, decades, centuries, and millennia. We come and go as individuals, plants and animals alike, but life goes on, to be experienced, and in the case of our species, enjoyed by those who follow, we hope.

...

Camposanto

I had searched our archives and found things that deepened my appreciation of her story. I learned that she had quite an unusual college experience considering her early life, perhaps with some parallels to her mother's time, brought up to mid-twentieth-century vintage. She was a good student and had high priorities for academic achievement but did so while reaching out for the socially broadening experience that anticipated the path she would follow in her post-college years.

She dated and mixed with people outside the pattern suggested by the cultural, ethnic, and religious uniformity of her hometown background. She spent time out of the university environment, sometimes weekending in Indianapolis, South Bend, and Chicago with friends including Jews, Eastern Europeans, Catholics, non-conformists, and intellectual strivers. One of her intriguing connections was with Dan Wakefield, who went on to be a successful novelist, screen writer, and academic. They had an on and off romantic relationship during the college years. When he moved on to New York, he wrote a couple of quite passionate notes to her, but absence didn't make the heart grow fonder on either side and their relationship ended.

Her older sister, Roena, had left Indiana University after her sophomore year and transferred to the University of New Mexico where she graduated and began teaching in the Albuquerque school system. There were long-standing family connections in New Mexico, and both girls had spent time there with older cousins and their families during their high school years. Chris felt the pull of New Mexico, and after graduation in 1954, she tried to follow Roena's lead and immediately take a teaching job there. The administrators there encouraged her to get a year of teaching under her belt in Indiana and then come to Albuquerque.

She followed that advice and accepted a post in the Frankfort school district in small-town Indiana. That year quickly convinced her to look for greener pastures. The rules for unmarried women teachers were strict and confining. Life was boring and narrowly constrained and lacking in stimulation. Teachers couldn't be seen drinking or smoking in public except at the local country club, and there were few opportunities for unregulated fun. It was a far cry from the freedom at the university in Bloomington. There were chances to connect with local bachelors, but the field was limited, and she couldn't imagine life in a small, provincial town. She escaped that existence and kept her eye on the New Mexico prize.

She joyfully accepted an Albuquerque teaching position and arrived in the booming post-war city to join her sister in a more adventurous place where the possibilities seemed endless. There were military bases with an abundance of young officers looking for young women for fun and maybe marriage, and she tried that path briefly before fate intervened. Everyone who knows us has heard the story of our meeting in the Triangle Bar. It was a place I had patronized in my earlier years as a student. The Triangle took its name from the shape of its lot, squeezed between the Albuquerque's main street, Central Avenue, and two other streets, right at the edge of the university campus. It had a long bar and tables for those who came for food, but for most of us it had been a place for beer. On that fateful evening we were served by Kate, a revered waitress, known to generations of students. It has always been a point of pride for us that we met in a saloon. On that first evening, after a brief introduction by her sister, Chris drove me back to my new home in the Student Union Building. She had a car. I didn't. I had just returned to the university after three years in the army and had been hired as the resident assistant manager of the facility.

That was September 1955, and it didn't take us long to decide we should go on together. It may have been as soon as October, when in a slightly woozy state after a pleasant evening together, I casually asked her if she thought we should maybe, sometime, want to think about getting married. She immediately brought me to my senses with her unequivocal challenge: "When?" Sixty years later we know how that question was answered. The "when?" became June 9, 1956, my twenty-sixth birthday, not many months after we met.

She was the yin to my yang. We were the opposites that attracted. She was conservative in the good sense. She protected, nurtured, and preserved the things that were important to her and us. She was initially reluctant to accept change but charged ahead when it became a reality in our lives. She was a self-described realist. On the other hand, I was impetuous, romantic, and a risk taker.

Chris and Harlan in 1957

Chris in Califonia 1975

Chris in 1988

We took the edge off each other's tendencies. I was inclined to be rash and impulsive. She was cautious and steady. She was even leery about our move from Albuquerque to Santa Fe when I graduated from law school, and how reasonable and "realistic" that resistance was. Why leave a booming, rapidly growing city and move to a small, insular state capital town where the prospects for a young lawyer seemed so limited? But there were big mountains and skiing, and I thought the sky was the limit.

But move we did, and many more times. We had eleven grand years in Santa Fe where I worked first as an Assistant Attorney General and then as the State's principle water lawyer. That last experience led me unexpectedly to a career with BP, British Petroleum, an international oil company that took us first to Alaska for four years, initially as lawyer and subsequently as an executive. In the lead up to the construction of The Alaska Pipeline, I worked closely with Alaska Natives, state government and national politicians to help ease the passage of the Native Claims Settlement Act, a prerequisite to building the pipeline. San Francisco followed, the company's U.S. headquarters, for three years, then Cleveland, Ohio. We had a short stint in Salt Lake City, in a frantic interval during which we had the daunting experience of owning four different houses in one year. We returned to Cleveland, bloodied but unbowed, and remained there until my retirement. It would be impossible to exaggerate the burden Chris carried as the logistical manager of our rambling lifestyle over those years. That tumultuous period came to an end with my retirement when we finally came back to our beloved Santa Fe. Over the twenty years we were away, my family and I maintained our close New Mexico connections with frequent visits. Even at a distance, we began our devoted commitment to the place we call the cabin.

During all our years together, Chris and I shared our decision making and most of the other demands of a busy, always changing lifetime, but there was no question she had to make the more challenging adjustments in our frenetic life, and she did it with zest, competence, energy, and skill. The accommodation to change, hunger for achievement, tenacity, and strength she learned in her childhood, teen, and college years made her ready for her role as a mother, wife, and an accomplished, multifaceted, card-carrying adult. We had a great time all those years, pigeonholing hard decisions and managing the difficult times along the way. That was all before the serious hard times of our last shared years.

Chris and Harlan in 1988

Chris and Harlan in 2010

My New Incarnation

We look back, but we live forward, and in my new incarnation, after Chris's death, I came to have the great good fortune to be accompanied by Lynn Day as I made my new beginning. The first few months of our joint venture followed a quite conventional path. She allowed me to play the male role of taking the social initiative for a while. After our first date for lunch in Santa Fe, there were other lunches and then an evening dinner or two. Our conversations were lively, and we enthusiastically enjoyed our times together. Then soon, Lynn's extensive social network came into play. I was invited to her grand annual summer dinner party, served in high style on her patio. I faced the challenge of meeting and remembering the names of a dozen of her diverse and interesting friends. The food and company were invigorating and unfamiliar to a man whose social life had been so restricted for years.

Since my social circle was so narrow compared to hers, I was able to reciprocate only with more frequent invitations for restaurant dinners and occasional drive-abouts for lunch in Madrid, Cerrillos, Las Vegas (the New Mexico one), and other exotic destinations. That arrangement gave us a chance to spend time as a couple, with opportunities to converse in quiet venues where two hearing-impaired people could carry on a conversation without having to guess what the other person was saying.

Over a period of a few months, we spent increasingly frequent times together, usually requiring her to elevate herself into the seat of my unfashionable truck for our jaunts. The evenings or afternoons would conclude with her gracefully bailing out of the truck, followed by a chaste kiss on the cheek at her front door. That said, we were having fun, alternating between her larger events and my more intimate ones, and, I hoped, ready for a more serious friendship. My singular life had been of brief duration at the time and I was enjoying our warm togetherness. I was beginning to wonder when it would be appropriate to invite her to visit my beloved cabin, but that would have to wait for a while.

...

It was a typical late August day for me, alone in the valley except for Baudelio and Frenchie. They had spent a frantic Friday trying to finish the windrowing, raking, baling, and loading of the last hay to be picked up that year. There were lots of problems. The windrower was broken and needed welding. The spear on the front of the loader used to pick up the bales was also out of commission. It was a typical harvest, with old equipment giving out under the pressure of getting the job done.

I started the morning with my chain saw in the meadow where a large branch had fallen during the last winter. I blocked up the fallen branch, cleaned up some of the smaller branches, and then noticed that Baudelio was across the river, trying to solve a mechanical problem. As I had been doing for decades, I strolled over to observe, understand the problem if I could, and see if there was anything I could do to help. As had been our practice over the years, there was no explanation from him of what was at issue, but it became clear he was trying to jerry-rig a solution to the bale-spear failure. Out of curiosity and willingness to help, I followed him across into the upper meadow where completed bales awaited pickup. The improvised solution didn't work, and we moved on to a more labor-intensive fallback option that involved me as the on-foot laborer for about four hours.

This scheme involved Baudelio thrusting the front end loader under the end of the 600-pound bale and securing the bale to the loader with a large strap, allowing him to carefully raise it up and carry it over to the old white truck that would be used to take the bales up Atencio Canyon, over the ridge, down the other side into Colorado, and on to Mogote where the bales would feed the cows in the coming winter. I helped guide him into position to lower the bales onto the truck.

We carried on in that fashion while Frenchie was running the baler, making the last hay ready to be picked up. Baudelio and I were running back and forth between bales and truck, he in the tractor, me on foot, hustling to complete the eight-bale load. There are always little adjustments to be made that Baudelio and I addressed with little verbal communication. We each had a comfortable sense of what the other needed to have happen and could usually anticipate the need.

When we were close to making the complete load ready for transit, an old blue jeep roared across the meadow, and an elderly couple emerged enthusiastically to greet Baudelio, addressing him as "Bud." They were old friends, retired farmers from eastern Colorado who summer here and winter in some warm place. The purpose of their visit today was to deliver the gift of a watermelon. Baudelio tried to show his appreciation for the gift while attempting to continue with his work. Finally, they left, and we pressed on.

It was close to 4:00 when the load was complete, and neither of us had had anything to eat all afternoon. That was not a big problem for me, but Baudelio, a diabetic, was at some risk. As he readied to drive off with his precarious load, he promised to stop for food "down below," meaning his nearby cabin. Relieved of duty, I recovered my ATV and headed back to my cabin for a late lunch and a little rest. A half hour later I saw Baudelio walking up the valley rather than driving over the ridge to Mogote. He explained, in his customary understated way, that "the darn truck has a flat tire." It was another problem to solve and a fitting way to end a difficult day.

The next day was another welcome hardworking one for me. I finished cutting up the remaining manageable parts of the huge limb in the meadow. It was a warm day, in the mid-eighties during the afternoon. After a good hot shower and a quiet dinner, I was on the porch, looking up at a new moon and the last faint, gray cloud decorating the mostly clear western sky. I had made my customary ATV circuit of my domain with a brief pause at the *camposanto* where, except for the dates on the bronze plaque, Chris's marker could have been there for decades or even a century.

The previous evening as I drove up the canyon and back, I came upon a young bear on the road just ahead of me. I paused to enjoy him. When he casually strolled off the road, I drove down to where he had disappeared, and there he was, about twenty feet up the hillside, standing up on his hind legs. We stared at each other for a moment, and I moved on as quietly as possible, in hopes of not disturbing him.

Aspen Grove

That evening as I was getting ready for bed, I went out to the porch for a last look, and standing there in the dark I became aware I was in the flight path of several bats who were circling around me in the soft glow of my porch light. I retreated, turned off the light, and the visitors soon left me alone.

At 8:30 a.m. it was a pleasant sixty degrees. Earlier that morning it had been thirty-eight. It's a stimulating contrast. It was the end of the weekend. The hay was in. The valley was bursting with the yellow and orange of autumn, mostly *chamisas* and sunflowers. It had been a busy time, this harvest rite; the trailing edge of more than a century of working people giving meaning to the place they called Santa Rita. I was keenly aware that the occupational use of the valley would soon be history, leaving it to its new part-time inhabitants to use and enjoy in our new and different ways.

Fall can be a melancholy time, a reminder of the winter to come and a natural metaphor for mortality. From an esthetic aspect, autumn can be the most inspiring season, a time of profound beauty and invigorating temperatures that encourage physical activity. A sunny, breezy day in October often had that influence on me. I recalled a day like that when I drove up the hill behind the cabin in search of aspen for my stove. I was able to provide fuel for my fires from fallen cottonwood trees on our property, but my favorite firewood is aspen. It's easy to split and burns clean.

There's a lovely little grove up the ridge where our frequent strong winds occasionally take down vulnerable trees, and on that trip, I found one that would provide me with a good half cord. The recently downed tree was green and very heavy, but the work was satisfying and exhausting. I loaded my truck, drove back down the rustic Forest Service road, and added the load to my tall and handsome wood pile. I was tired and pleasantly used up, happy to decline an invitation from a neighbor for a glass of wine and glad for quiet time on my own at the end of a blustery day.

The next day was better; still breezy but warmer. I did quite a bit of reading; Chimamanda Addichie's *Americanah*, the sad story of a Nigerian woman dealing with her problems in a difficult foreign country, America. I spent more time with Montaigne, the first modern man, born in sixteenth-century France and maybe the first hippie.

Santa Rita is hard for me in a way, because Chris has more presence there than she does on West San Francisco Street, my new home in Santa Fe. There are constant reminders. Those memory moments are okay most of the time, and the place is such a miracle that it overwhelms the downside emotions. That morning, I rode my ATV up the valley to the steep rise, up towards my friend, Ken Bateman's cabin. The bright yellow aspen dots are like daylight candles scattered through the dark green ponderosa and spruce fabric of the mountain sides. The cottonwoods, shimmering yellow and orange, produced their own incandescent energy, and the river's voice was querulous and insistent, way beyond its usual gentle October whisper.

At the end of an uplifting day, it was time for bed and the exaggerated silence that comes with removing hearing aids, shutting out the sound of bugling elk, maybe howling coyotes, and surely the sound of the laboring old refrigerator. The next day, it was back to Santa Fe and the other side of my life.

A couple of weeks later, it was time again for end of the season chores at the cabin. It was a windy, cool day when I hooked up the trailer to take my riding mower three miles down the rough road to the village of San Miguel and my friend Peter Shoenfeld's barn for winter storage. He had cooked a nice green chile stew for lunch. Back at the cabin a bit later, I saw Baudelio and Frenchie going down the road with the backhoe, taking it to Mogote for the winter. Things were buttoning up in Santa Rita. Another friend, Jimmie Van Soelen, was still there. Jimmie was our town crier, always having a story to tell about goings on. That day he reported he had watched a bald eagle dive bombing a couple of red tailed hawks and then saw an osprey circle around, land in a big ponderosa by the river, and spend forty minutes eating a trout he had just caught.

Back at the cabin there were still lots of reminders of Chris. I got rid of the last old deck of cards with "Chris" written on the box cover and found an envelope with the words "Shed Keys" written in her recognizable script. She had written a message inside the breaker box reading, "Do not turn on water heater until tank is full of water!" There are dozens of her bird books, a tall tumbler full of her blue glass, a vase full of her special rocks, her Cleveland Indians cap, and the Amish church bench.

Later, it was a lovely fall afternoon and I helped Baudelio take down a fence that crossed the river in front of his cabin. It was there to keep the cows out of the irrigated meadow, but the cow season was over. We were in the river for over an hour, pulling staples out of fence posts, laying aside the posts and rolling up barbed wire. Baudelio did the rolling. He's been doing that for about seventy years, saving old wire for another year. When we came out of the river, I noticed a roll of rusty wire hanging in a bush that had been laid aside in an earlier year. As we worked in the river, Baudelio occasionally took off a glove to retrieve a staple from the stream bed and put it in his shirt pocket. Waste not.

When we finished, I took my ATV through the river to the south side, drove along the acequia above our meadow, still flowing to keep the field moist and encourage next year's growth, then up the *chamisa* covered hillside to the *camposanto* and Chris's marker. I do that from time to time and always remember that we were often there together over the years, in the truck in recent times after she decided the back of the ATV was a bad idea. It's a great view back to the cabin side of the river through the cottonwoods, without their leaves by then. There was not a breath of wind, and it was silent except for the gentle river sound. When we were together there, it was inescapable that we would think of our ultimate return there permanently, some day in the unthreatening future. It was not a worrying thought.

As usual that time of year, I was the only person in the valley after Baudelio headed back to Mogote. The whole canyon was empty of people, all the way up to the last cabin and the steep rise to the Toltec Gorge, where the river cascades down its precipitous course from almost a thousand feet above. I often thought how different this long valley must have been in the early twentieth century when it was bustling with the people of Santa Rita, including those in its upper reaches, who called their part of the neighborhood *Los Crestones*, named after the rocky outcrops above their cabins.

That morning I had taken a slow ride up the river, just to savor the scene. I stopped on the steep hill up to the Bateman cabin, turned off the engine, and looked out at the stunning meadow, craggy cliffs, and forested steeps surrounding the junction of Lobo Creek and the *Rio de Los Pinos*. Don Mullin's cabin stood out at the edge of the meadow with its tattered American flag standing at attention in the breeze. The area surrounding the merger of the two streams glistened brightly, reflecting the morning sun shining on the acres of wetlands above the dams built by the busy beavers. On the viewpoint where I paused, I was surrounded by gigantic ponderosas and spruce, some old enough to have been there when the place was used seasonally by its earlier occupants, the Utes, Navajos, and Apaches. The place now marks an outer edge of what was the Hispano homeland for a moment in geologic time, after being enjoyed for many centuries by the original Americans.

Back on my porch with the lengthening shadows of late afternoon, I listened to the river, the visiting *piñon* jays and the resident stellar jays competing at the feeder. What a privilege and joy it was to be there; a transient human, enjoying the gift of being a temporary occupant of this special little world, remote from the hustle of the other world, comfortable in the warm sun of the high country and ready to retreat to the warm cabin in a few minutes. The sun was still above the high hill, and when I looked directly down from the sun to the river, I saw its shimmering reflection on the rippling surface of the stream.

I could feel the approaching chill and snapped my down vest closed. The jays were feeding as if there would be no tomorrow. The shadows were at the fence line and creeping up toward me. My beer was warm and almost gone. It was time to move in, time for a fire in the wood stove.

The year was coming to an end, and we hoped the snows would come soon and prevent all but the most persistent humans from sharing the place with its other residents until an uncertain date in the spring. There would be more city time with Lynn, chamber music concerts, settling into my new house. It was well into another autumn and time for another lunch stop in Ojo Caliente on the way South. Nora Bustos was serving. Like Tony Chacón, she's also a resident of El Rito, some twenty miles away, but works at the cafe on weekends. As is the case with many *norteñas*, she works whenever she can, doing extra time to supplement their modest family income and counter the economic insecurity of so many people in rural northern

New Mexico. Unlike the romantic, magical, picaresque stories of Tony Chacón,, Nora's are sometimes from the darker side of *El Norte* and especially Rio Arriba and Taos Counties. But I'm getting ahead of myself and should let Nora tell her own story.

She's a warm and cheerful woman who always greets me with a smile and a hug, a welcome she shares with most of the people who drop in for a meal and good conversation. She is often joined by her husband, Ricky, a great bear of a man, often wearing a billed cap that marks him as an army veteran, a retired master sergeant. Ricky sometimes works in the kitchen washing dishes and helping with whatever else needs doing. I've met their son, also a Ricky, who was then a senior in college at New Mexico State University at the other end of the state in Las Cruces. He has since graduated, but was then a student in the Agriculture Department, preparing to be a county agricultural agent or a teacher when he graduated—career paths that could provide him with employment in his home region which is plagued with a very high unemployment rate.

Before I heard this story, Nora had told me about her plans for Thanksgiving when she would be hosting a gigantic group of thirty-plus people, mostly family. In these parts, almost everyone is family to some degree. The people of these little villages have lived together and shared their genes for centuries. The merger of families has made for an extraordinary web of relationships and a real sense of community.

This is the story she told me. Son Ricky had come home for the Thanksgiving feast and it was a happy time for all. Nora said he had spent the Friday after Thanksgiving visiting with his best friend who had been a classmate in high school. They had laughed together and told stories about their school years and friends. Ricky left on the weekend to return to Las Cruces.

Nora calmly said to me, "I had to call Ricky on Tuesday to tell him his best friend had committed suicide the day before." I said, "Oh my God. How horrible. Did Ricky say that his friend had been acting strangely?" She said that no, he had seemed happy and just like his old self. He even had a job, but like so many other jobs in Espanola, it wasn't leading to anything. She said, "This happens all the time."

Between serving tables and carrying dirty dishes back to the kitchen, Nora told me about the tragic deaths of other young people she knew. One was an overdose. Another was an alcohol related motorcycle accident. The one that touched her most deeply was that of a beautiful, brilliant young Hispana woman she knew from Chimayo. She was only twenty-seven and in the final stages of completing her PhD, working on her dissertation, Nora said, when without warning she killed herself. There was no explanation. "What a terrible waste," she said.

On her next trip back from the kitchen, Nora said, "Told my son I'm glad he got away from here."

GOLDEN DAYS

It was the eighth day of January, the unofficial first day of the year, a few days after the exhilarating experience of watching my daughter, Tina Smith, sworn in as the Junior United States Senator from Minnesota. I declared this odd date as the beginning of the New Year because I was reading *The Sum of Our Days* by Isabel Allende and she informed her readers that she always begins writing her next book on January 8. Could that work for me? I knew I would surely fall far short of her accomplishment. And her book was a memoir, a genre that gave her another distinct advantage. She could call on the history of a really fucked up family as source material for her amazing tales. My family stories are more commonplace, and our family tragedies and challenges don't hold a candle to hers.

My initial January 8 stumbling block, unlike Allende's, was the lack of a plan, a plot, a cast of characters, and I couldn't fall back on a reservoir of research, deep thought, and inspiration such as launched her great books. My modest project, if it even took root, would have to begin with apologetic lines, the search for a reason to write and a path to follow. With the examples of Allende and Tina Smith as my spur, I would have to ignore writer's block, begin to write, and wait for some modest direction to reveal itself, making it seem worthwhile to continue.

It was a new year, and I was in the second year of my restart. My handsome partner, Lynn, was making it a good departure from my old routine. With her encouragement, we were booked to hear concerts by the Escher Quartet and the Santa Fe Symphony in January. The ski season was barely starting because of the lack of snow. The dry weather even made it possible for me to have two nights at the cabin, an almost unprecedented opportunity for that time of year. It was cold but snowless, but a comforting, silent interlude for me. The river was frozen, dampening its familiar melody. Back in town, I was reinventing myself with exercise at the gym and a first try at meditation.

...

After the gym on our first snowy day, I'm home to my online meditation program. My mysterious, invisible guide tells me:

"Rather than trying to think of something, just see what the mind comes up with."

I'm trying to think about what that message means. It's hard to step back from the mind and let it do what it wants to do. Is it possible that my mind has a mind of its own? This gets confusing and gives me mind cramps. After all, the mind is our tool, and we feel that somehow it responds to what we want it to do. The paradox, of course, is that it is our mind that lets us have the delusion that we are in control. Okay, I'm going to relax and give it a try.

The process of meditation does free the mind from its impulse to overthink things and to randomly shift focus, sometimes impulsively, from thing to thing. The conscious effort to rest the mind, encouraged in meditation, may allow one to escape the matters that normally occupy the mind and make space for new thoughts and ideas that are otherwise crowded out.

In most of my recent meditation sessions, in a package devoted to creativity, I've been instructed to think of a brilliant creative spark inside my chest that is expanding rapidly outward in every direction to a distance that is beyond my capacity to imagine. That would seem to be infinity, a distance with no end, no boundary; the beyond, beyond the beyond. That invites me to zoom back from that outer edge without edge, to the inner space, that very small space where I sit before my computer. Am I overthinking this? I look up from my yellow pad to see that the computer says I have accumulated nine hundred and sixteen minutes of meditation and that I have meditated four days in a row. That's not much in the context of infinity, but it's a good start and something for my mind to think about.

···

The Escher Quartet had been an amazing escape from the shit-hole president. The musicians took us out of our drab, unsettled world and into the breathtaking experience of listening and watching. Seeing as well as listening to performing musicians adds to our appreciation of the complexity and subtlety of their skill.

A great string quartet is a miracle, the amazing virtuosity of the individual players, the blending of such different but related instruments, the communication between the performers. The product almost seems to be produced by one instrument played by four artists. It brought tears to my eyes and gave me hope for the other world from which we were taking a brief vacation. We were reminded that the long-term impact of Beethoven, Haydn, and even the lesser known Kurtag, will be greater than that of even strong presidents. That helps offset the disaster of our present leader.

It is a special pleasure to enjoy music with Lynn, who is a knowledgeable listener with insights derived from her years of semi-professional work with the Metropolitan Opera, where she organized west coast auditions for singers. Music is one of our most enjoyable shared activities, and whether we are in formal venues or in our casual daily routine, she always looks great. I struggle to define Lynn's appearance. I'm proud to be seen with her. She is probably not described as beautiful but she's certainly elegant. She's tall, slender, and graceful, and dresses in ways that enhance her impact. In a room full of people, she will always be noticed.

We were having fun. I was adjusting to her lifestyle and she was accommodating mine. Her circle of friends was broad. Mine was narrow. Her social group's entertainment included cocktail parties. Mine centered on quiet getaways, and the cabin. It worked. Our previous lives had been very different. She and her husband had an intriguing history. Right out of college, she had been a night shift reporter for the Philadelphia *Bulletin* and met her husband, Tony Day, there. After their marriage they moved to Washington where he was in the Washington Bureau for the *Bulletin* and later was its White House correspondent. This high-profile experience led to his recruitment as Editorial Page Editor for the *Los Angeles Times* at the time when newspapers were at the peak of their power and influence. While in Washington, she and Tony were in professional and social engagement with the political aristocracy. That included Henry Kissinger, who later engaged Tony as editor for much of his later writings. They became friends despite their sharply conflicting political positions. The Days met and had family visits with Jimmy Carter, Lyndon Johnson, and other luminaries.

As mentioned, after eleven years in Santa Fe, spent mostly in state government with a brief stint in private law practice, I had been a corporate executive in Big Oil, working twenty years for BP, a global company. That provided me international experience including a stint in South Africa in the closing years of apartheid, where I had the honor of meeting Bishop Tutu. My corporate portfolio was varied and included environmental affairs, government relations and community relations. In my later years there I was responsible for managing the BP's corporate philanthropy. Lynn and I traded stories and smiles about our business and social networks. We often marveled at the changes we had experienced in our nearly century-long lives.

As we entered a new year my thoughts often returned to Baudelio. My annual first visit with him had already signaled the arrival of spring. Looking back, it often occurred to me that our friendship would not have been predicted. We could hardly have come from more dissimilar places. He was born at home in San Miguel, New Mexico, on January 30, 1941, in a little house with no electricity or running water, with the help of a *partera*, a midwife. I was born in Providence, Rhode Island, on June 9, 1930, in a modern hospital, with the help of an obstetrician, and returned home to a contemporary house with all the conveniences of the day. He was born into a family of subsistence farmers and stockmen of Hispanic heritage who had only modest formal education and spoke little or no English. I was born into a family where both parents were college educated. They were both of English heritage, and English was the only language spoken in our home.

Baudelio's family homes during his growing up years, sometimes changing seasonally between summer and winter, were modest, rustic, handmade structures with no modern conveniences and heated with simple wood burning stoves. We lived in substantial suburban houses with all the comforts and accessories of modern life. He lived in a small Hispano world where the majority Anglo society was at the outer edge of his consciousness. I lived in the middle of the majority Anglo world, unaware of the existence of any other culture.

I pondered these contrasts while sitting close to the warm stove in my straw bale cabin on a cold winter night on the edge of the wilderness, forty-five minutes from a paved road and right next door to the little adobe house where Baudelio's family lived seventy years before. It was that circumstance that had brought us together over forty years earlier. When I came to that place and met Baudelio, we began the faltering, uneasy establishment of a relationship, struggling to find common ground and careful to avoid breaches of etiquette in our cross-cultural engagement.

English was still his second language and my Spanish was academic and conversationally iffy. Despite our initial unease and tentativeness, we gave each other the benefit of the doubt and gradually came to be more comfortable and unselfconscious. We became great friends, teaching each other valuable lessons from our separate histories and perspectives. We overcame, or perhaps better said, benefited, from our diversity, and our coming together as friends has been a gift. We speak the same language in different languages.

The unfortunate lack of snow in the previous winter made it possible for me to visit Santa Rita in late January, much earlier than normal. I invited Baudelio to join me for an overnight, giving me a welcome chance to spend more time with him than usual. Looking back, I realize it may have been the last lengthy conversation we would have. We had dinner, a couple of beers for him, a couple of glasses of wine for me, and were sitting in the warm cabin talking about family history, remembering Santa Rita anecdotes and exchanging random thoughts. We had known each other for decades, but like most men, had not often shared deep personal thoughts about what I hesitate to call our philosophy of life, or even more risky, our religious views. But it was a good discussion of things that happened in Santa Rita and the people who are our neighbors there. We shared opinions on what might be called moral or ethical issues that arise from time to time in any neighborhood. When Baudelio agreed with something I had said, he endorsed my comments with a firm "amen."

After a thoughtful pause, he asked, "What do you believe about the afterlife?" I paused to get my thoughts in order. It's a touchy issue and I didn't want to offend.

Lets look at the bright side. Baudelio and Maria

I knew he attended a conservative Protestant Hispanic church in Antonito and assumed he probably had a pretty literal concept of heaven as the preferred afterlife destination. I didn't want to distance myself from him with an answer that would challenge or reject his beliefs, but I wanted to be honest with him and not pretend our views were convergent. I fell back on euphemism and metaphor, the coward's way out, and said something along these lines.

"I think that when any individual living thing dies, plant or animal, including humans, that individual being disappears permanently, but it lives on in the next generation of its species. After the hay is mowed in your meadows in the fall, it dies, but new life returns in the spring. When you send your steers to be butchered in the fall, the individual animals die, but the herd is reborn in the spring. I think the same thing is true of human beings. As individuals, we live and die, but we are replaced by our children and our grandchildren, and we live on through them."

Nice try. And my actual response was probably not that cogent. After that dodgy little lecture, I asked Baudelio what he believed. He thought about it and tried to put his ideas into words, struggling, I'm guessing, both with what he believed and how to express it in English. What he came up with seemed to be a very nice compromise between our quite different beliefs. He said, "I don't think I will see Arlene again, but I think our spirits are still alive after we die. Our spirits are still here." Maybe not an exact quote, but it's close enough. I told him I thought that was a very good way to describe it and was a way I could agree with completely. The spirit of a person we have loved lives on in our memory and consciousness. At times we even seem to hear the voice of that spirit, perhaps in the middle of the night. Baudelio said he still hears Arlene's voice. I told him I hear Chris's voice too. Having concluded our ecclesiastical discussion, we enjoyed a few more quiet moments around our wood-fired stove, stretched and yawned, decided that enough was enough for the evening, and headed off to bed.

In the morning, I told Baudelio about the new woman in my life, and with his cryptic wisdom, he responded, "Two is better than one." This was another parallel in our lives, because he too had an important woman friend in his life, who had appeared serendipitously several years before.

In his high school years, Baudelio had a challenge that was common for the families living in remote, rural areas like Santa Rita. It was impossible to attend the closest high school in Antonito. The commute would have taken over an hour each way, even if the family owned a vehicle capable of making the trip. With the help of an unexplained miracle, it became possible for him to become a boarding student at the McCurdy School in Española. McCurdy was an institution that served a significant number of mostly Hispano students who could not otherwise complete high school because of their remote family homes. Maria Martinez's family lived in Dixon, another mostly Hispano community with the same disadvantage. Baudelio and Maria were in the same class at McCurdy, didn't really know each other well, and soon went their separate ways. They each married, had children, and, in her case, grandchildren, and never saw one another until a second miracle reintroduced them.

Baudelio had never had a vacation in the many years he shared with Arlene. There was no money, and the demands of their small, interstate farm and ranch business made it impossible to get away. Then the second miracle happened. Baudelio signed up for a bus tour that would take him to Branson, Missouri. Branson is a resort created as a fundamentalist Christian community, perhaps representative of the conservative beliefs of Baudelio's church in Antonito. In any event, it provided him with a stimulating week of unfamiliar fun and entertainment. Maria and a group of friends had boarded the same bus in Española, and Baudelio joined the tour in Antonito. To their mutual surprise, they recognized one other and Baudelio joined their party. It was a magical week for him—theatre every night, being a tourist every day, and getting reacquainted with this active and stimulating widow. Baudelio had never seen live theatre and he was inspired.

After the trip, the two new, old acquaintances began to see each other regularly in Mogote and Dixon, trading visits that included introducing Maria to Santa Rita. They were good company, became friends, and he shared other vacation trips with Maria and her friends, including a memorable evening at the Grand Ole Opry in Nashville. So, we two old widowers had found two charming old widows to brighten our days.

It had been a slow winter with little skiing opportunity, and the spring and summer were languid and enjoyable, but it had been a busy time for me, not least for all the things Lynn and I did together. We heard two more splendid string quartet performances. We met Xochitl Torres Small, an inspiring young Democratic candidate for Congress from the district in southern New Mexico, who went on to win by a tiny margin in November. We attended three funerals for old friends of mine. I helped my daughter-in-law Nicole move her office. I flew to Washington to hear my daughter give her maiden speech on the Senate floor and wondered what it had to do with "maidens." She emphasized her already productive efforts to reach across the aisle to find common ground with Republican Senators. We went to the Seventeenth Annual Weed Bluegrass Festival in Weed, New Mexico. Lynn and I attended the Santa Fe Opera twice; once to see and hear *Doctor Atomic*, thematically born in neighboring Los Alamos. And I spent many hours with Steve O'Neill, my computer guru, straightening out me and my computer. I memorialized another winter happening.

My Santa Fe house is full of hardworking Hispanic guys. They're here to replace my failed heating system. I call them Hispanics because they're not locals, not Hispanos. The head guy is Amos Saenz, a big, slightly overweight guy who came here from Mexico about twenty years ago. Everyone in the five-man crew speaks Spanish, including the local electrician who showed up this afternoon. They all work hard, and everyone sounds happy. The house is filled with laughter and storytelling as they work. I can't fully enjoy the stories in Spanish, but then again, I often fail to hear the stories told in English with my bad hearing. I'm sure at least some of the men are undocumented or illegal, as Trump would emphasize.

Amos has a small business called High Desert Air Conditioning and Heating. I was referred to him by one of the long-established plumbing and heating firms during a busy Christmas season in 2015 when both furnaces in our house crashed the day before Christmas. His wife was the phone contact and Amos showed up immediately. We shared a cordial conversation about my problem. He diagnosed our problems and determined that our first furnace was dead. The second furnace was still workable but had asbestos in the connection to the air ducts. That problem needed to be fixed, and we decided that because of its age and the cost of repairs, a new furnace would be the safest and most cost-efficient way to go. Two new furnaces. Merry Christmas.

Amos and his all Mexican crew showed up on Christmas Eve morning, worked into the evening, and had both new furnaces up and running by nine o'clock, at a reasonable price and rescuing our Christmas gathering. As is my habit, I liked him and trusted him immediately. I'm seldom disappointed when I judge and trust people quickly, and I'm happy to be occasionally disappointed rather than withhold trust until it's absolutely proven to be deserved.

Two years later, with a failed boiler in my new house, Amos and his happy crew are here again to get me back in business. Bright and early this morning, they were on the job and the work was soon finished. It was an unhappy necessity, but a pleasure to watch and listen to the sound of my money going out the door. Amos and his guys are good people, well skilled or learning on the job from each other with constant animated conversation. They were happy in their work, careful with the house, good-humored, and they filled the house with the music of Spanish voices. It revived my faith in mankind to have them here. They are an example to emulate and having them here informed my opinions on the immigration debate.

...

A more enjoyable interlude in the winter of my discontent was an invitation from Lynn to join her for the first meeting of a series of lectures that were devoted to Marcel Proust's sprawling novel, *Swann's Way*. In preparation for that event, I read the first one hundred pages of the book, a small chunk of its first thousand pages. And that was just the first volume of his massive work.

At this early stage of my reading, I had only these tentative observations. First, Proust seemed to have had a very peculiar, dare I say unhealthy, relationship

Lynn Day and F Harlan Flint

with his mother. Second, the stream of his consciousness seems to be out of its banks. His powers of description are awesome and sometimes overwhelming. In one famous passage, he exhausted two pages and some of his readers, describing the sensations he experienced while tasting a spoonful of tea and a crumb of cake. Third, he seems to suffer from what could be generously described as emotional excess. For example, in describing the intense sense of loss he felt on being temporarily separated from his mother, he said it brought him, "of a sudden to a sort of puberty of sorrow and a manumission of tears."

My online meditation guide had encouraged me "to be mindful throughout the day," so I was mindful of the likelihood that I was underestimating and mischaracterizing the great Marcel Proust. To test my preconceptions of Proust, I signed up for the rest of the Proust classes.

As my friendship with Lynn warmed and we became more comfortable together, I began to realize that I was actually courting her, wanting more of her time and feeling a deeper affection, but I was cautious not to push the boundaries too far, not knowing how she felt or how I felt , for that matter. The good night kiss began to be accompanied by a hug, still very restrained and prosaic by today's standards; an experience that took me back about seventy years. By the subtle signals that mark these relationships, I thought her feelings were the same as mine. She welcomed the help of my hand as we walked in the dark to my truck or to a restaurant, and we held hands at times when it wasn't necessary.

Finally, one night as I was leaving her with a kiss at her front door, she said, "Goodnight, my love." Those were the first words uttered by either of us that suggested we might be moving along to a new level, and I was deeply moved by what she had said, but not enough to respond at the moment, as I walked back to my truck. I overcame my caution and it didn't take long for this twentieth century man to catch up with his twenty first century woman. We soon decided we were partners. This was obviously a life-changing event, but we moved on in more prosaic ways too. Prompted by my new state of being and the recognizing I needed to do what was necessary to sustain it for as long as possible, I stepped up my sessions at the gym and recorded my thoughts.

It's March of 2018, and I'm creeping up on the seventieth anniversary of my high school graduation. I'm at the gym bright and early; about the same weight (175 lbs.) and one inch shorter (72 inches) than when I was an uninspiring left end on a miserable high school football team. But here I am, still trying to keep the old machine running.

Start with table squat press; two repetitions of ten. Ooh, it hurts, but I'm doing it.

Next, table step up—kind of a pushup, going from elbows up to extended arms. Two reps. of twelve. Hard, but I can do it.

Next exercise: long strap row; two reps. of fifteen. Not too bad. Next, leg press. Really burns.

Next: leg curl; three reps. of twenty-five. Gotta go slow and bring legs back all the way. No cheating. Ouch.

Thinking about my up-north cabin and my aging friend Baudelio. Diabetes makes it tough, and he's having some dizzy spells and maybe some memory problems. Sounded good on the phone yesterday. Wobbled on to next station.

Roman torture (my terminology). Two reps. of twenty (maybe). Hurts like hell and makes me walk funny when I'm done.
Where the hell do I go from here?

Next exercise—knee tucks. Three reps. of twenty-five. Hard work, but starts in supine position on table, so time for a little rest and meditation.

I let my mind rest. Doing the exercises is a lot like meditation. Focus on the effort. Push through pain. The mind distracted from external reality, followed by the deep relief and pleasure of sinking into the resting body. The knee tucks really hurt, but it's the last exercise, and the finish line is in sight.

Finally, a series of stretches that we hope will sustain or maybe even improve bodily function. It's time now to move on to everyday life.

...

It was a gray day in Santa Fe, cold and spitting snow; the kind of day that brightens the consciousness of a *Santafesino*, like a sunbreak cheers a Seattleite after forty uninterrupted days of rain. That's what my Seattle son had reported recently. It was Sunday and I was back in my truck after a latte at my favorite coffee place and was greeted on the satellite radio by the solemn and majestic first measures of the Verdi *Requiem*. I couldn't bear the thought of going straight home and cutting short the music. On the spur of the moment, I headed north on the interstate, committed to not turning around until the requiem had concluded. It lifted my spirits all the way to the Chama River crossing, north of Española. Having gone that far on this familiar route, I decided to push on to the Mesa Vista Café, accompanied along the way by a Mozart string trio.

Sunday was a good day for a requiem, and the Verdi is one of the grandest, acquiescing as it does to the reality of death but proclaiming and gloriously celebrating the possibility of immortality, one of mankind's most enduring delusions. As I drove north, the dark sky fell like a curtain over the road, and sifting snow became a mini blizzard, a grand natural reflection of the music. The mood lightened as I entered the restaurant and was greeted with a hug by Nora. She had turned in my regular order for a red chile cheese enchilada plate with onions as soon as she saw me come through the door. I was also greeted by the owner, Leonel, and

Kaila, who was cooking that day. Ricky, Nora's husband, was also there, helping in the kitchen.

After a leisurely lunch, I said my goodbyes and drove back south, humming along with the sumptuous melodies of Brahms' Symphony no. 3. The fallow fields along the Rio Ojo Caliente had been dusted with snow. I noticed the big wood piles, stacked next to and sometimes almost matching the size of the small farmhouses. The wood piles are a nostalgic symbol of the human persistence required to survive in this harsh and unforgiving landscape where people earn only marginal livings.

After Brahms, I made the rest of my way home with a lively Tchaikovsky string quartet. My mind went back to the monumental Verdi that I hoped would never end, even if I had to drive on to Denver.

I had the same feeling two weeks ago after a performance of the Beethoven String Quartet in F Major, op. 135. It was his last string quartet, a strikingly modern, inventive piece, written, miraculously, long after he had lost the ability to hear his music performed. After hearing it live, I commented to my Lynn that I would gladly hear that music every morning for the rest of my life and never tire of it. Great music is the window to our heart.

The readings we did for the Proust lectures and other books I had been enjoying seemed to converge on one fundamental phenomenon of the human condition. It was "Love, Oh Love, Oh Careless Love." It was a subject close to my heart as Lynn and I were beginning our own affair of the heart. The word, its definition, and connotations have been the fascination of philosophers, poets, novelists, and the rest of us throughout time. As chance would have it, I was enjoying three literary encounters with this intriguing subject.

The first was with Sarah Bakewell's *How to Live: Or a Life of Montaigne.* In her delightful revisiting of the life of Michel de Montaigne, she provided answers to the issues raised by the title, including one asking how to "Survive Love and Loss." I was still dealing with surviving loss. It hadn't occurred to me that love was something to survive. A subheading for that chapter provided a hint: "La Boétie: Love and Tyranny." Montaigne and Etienne de La Boétie became acquainted as young men, probably in the 1550s. Their affection for one another was manifested in their writings to and about each other. Bakewell gave examples of how they described their love. La Boétie: "You have been bound to me, Montaigne, both by the power of nature and by virtue, which is the sweet allurement of love." Montaigne in turn wrote, "If you press me to tell why I loved him, I feel that this cannot be expressed, except by answering: Because it was he, because it was I."

Bakewell reminds us that, "The Renaissance was a period in which, while any hint of real homosexuality was regarded with horror, men routinely wrote to each other like lovesick teenagers." They were not so much in love with each other, she suggests, as with the philosophical concept of love they derived from Greek and Roman writings, and particularly those describing the relationship between Socrates and his young friend, Alcibiades. But perhaps there was some deep affection or even physical attraction between them.

Unfortunately, La Boétie died quite young, and Montaigne grieved his loss intensely for many years. Both men were married and had children, but there seems to be no evidence that their love for their wives and children rose to the stratospheric level of their love for each other. Love unfulfilled but described rhapsodically seems to have been the love suffered by Montaigne. It was apparently a love that he did not survive.

A second literary adventure with love came from the first volume of Marcel Proust's *Swann's Way*, "In Search of Lost Time. Remembrance of Things Past," a majestic effort that could be described as telling the story of Proust himself and his place in the society he inhabited during France's Belle Epoch. My own rather long sentence may have been provoked by Proust's pattern of producing extraordinarily long sentences and paragraphs that could go on for pages. He was not short of words.

We learned in the lecture series supporting our reading of *Swann's Way* that Proust was an open homosexual, and it is likely he observed love through that prism. During his time, homosexuality was widely accepted, accommodated or tolerated by society more than it has been in our time, but it probably still carried some level of stigma and disapproval.

In *Swann's Way*, we watch with fascination the self-inflicted torture of the title character as he subjectively describes and suffers the pangs of love he feels for Odette, the demimonde object of his passion. The agony accompanying his grand attraction is always most intense when he is out of her presence, and his real feelings for the object of his love become increasingly negative as the relationship approaches its consummation with their marriage. Their sexual consummation had occurred long before, but that physical bond seems to have been almost incidental and inconsequential.

Swann's love for Odette was self-generated, with little or no kindling by their actual real-life interaction. They had little in common. Their conversations were stilted and barren. One wonders if Proust, a revealed gay man himself, was not almost projecting himself into the character and describing the doomed effort of a gay man to find a deep and passionate love for a woman.

That's two down; two examples, by chance, of openly gay or possibly gay writers who experienced love or described it in ways that fall short of what one would hope love might mean. Theirs were certainly bleak experiences with love, and their view of love was at best ambiguous, tainted perhaps by the unique challenges of same-sex love. We can agree that homosexual men should have the same capacity to enjoy love and describe it for readers as heterosexual men, but there can be no doubt that society places barriers to that possibility.

My third random sample was provided by a chance encounter with a sixteenth-century luminary who revealed himself in a most unexpected way. I was given a glimpse at love through the eyes of a philosopher who appeared to me on a bookshelf at Lynn's house. I was providing emotional support as she made the difficult decision to dispose of some volumes in the large collection she and her husband had accumulated over many decades. While she agonized, I pulled out a small dusty book and found it was inscribed on the inside cover: "Clinton A. Cilley. Harvard 1857." Before looking at the title of the book, I learned from Lynn that Clinton Cilley was her great-grandfather who fought for the Union in the Civil War and earned the Congressional Medal of Honor, but that's another story.

As it turned out, the book was *Bacon's Essays and Wisdom of the Ancients*. Google later reminded me that Francis Bacon (1561–1626) was a flamboyant gay, the father of empiricism, who believed that scientific knowledge derives from inductive reasoning and observation of events in nature. Would you believe that all three sources on my unscientifically derived reading list would turn out to be gay? What are the chances? So, my sample is flawed and will invalidate any conclusions I might try to reach. That means I will have to broaden my sample and read much more before reaching any reliable answers about love. As if that weren't bad enough, I opened the Bacon book to see if he had anything to say on the subject of love, and to my dismay, discovered that he did. From reading his own words on the subject, I can only conclude that he was an unrelenting misanthrope and a serious pain in the ass. Let his words speak for themselves. I struggled with the archaic English of the text, but this is what I learned:

> *"The Stage is more beholding to LOVE than The Life of Man. For as to the stage, LOVE is even a matter of Comedies, and now and then of Tragedies, but in life, it doth much mischief, sometimes like a Syren, sometimes like a Fury. You may observe that amongst all the great and worthy Persons, there is not One that hath been transported to the mad degree of LOVE: that shows that great spirits...do keep out this weak passion. It seems (though rarely) that LOVE can find entrance, not only into an open heart, but also into a Heart well fortified if watch be not well kept."*

What a sad detour this has been through three wintry visions of this warmest of human conditions. These three guides left me with disappointment and a vigorous dissenting opinion. I'm back to the books in search of much sunnier views on this beloved subject.

A Long Goodbye, with Distractions

The spring and summer of the year provided both new and old scenarios. The new were the mostly Santa Fe based activities generated by Lynn's place in my life. The old were the decades old pattern of round trips to Santa Rita. The only noticeable change in routine at the cabin was the obvious decline in Baudelio's ability to maintain his ancient role as farmer and rancher. He was still there regularly and seemed almost as indestructible as he had ever been, but it took him longer to complete the tasks he had always done. The cows seemed to have sensed his inability to control their grazing behavior. They are amazingly strong-willed creatures and always find ways to be where they want to be rather than where the rest of us want them to be. It was harder for Baudelio to maintain and repair the ancient fences, and "changing the water," as he called it, required endless hours along the acequias and sub-ditches to keep the water where it was intended to be. I have already described the adventure of keeping old machinery and equipment operational. The will was still there, but the body was letting him down.

One of the services he had been providing for many years to our collection of part-time property owners in the valley was keeping the rough road navigable to the properties on up the five-mile-long valley. He had always been a skilled equipment operator on his backhoe. However, in that last summer he seemed to be more accident prone, and we were all concerned about his ability to continue that dangerous work. His family encouraged him to let Frenchie take on those tasks, but he insisted he could do it himself.

Diabetes was taking its toll, and he was struggling to manage his insulin. That challenge was compounded by what we all perceived to be occasional memory lapses. His daughter, Sandra, and Frenchie were devoted to him, and she tried to supervise his medical routine, but he was a stubborn, independent man and resisted being managed. Their houses in Mogote were side by side, and he didn't resist joining them for the good food Frenchie prepared, probably a much more balanced diet than he had been used to most of his life. So, the times they were a-changing, and all his friends were regretfully anticipating the end of an era that began with his father in the early 1950s when the first Anglo newcomers started to arrive.

For my part, it was especially poignant because of our close ties. I did what I could to lend a hand and keep an eye on him when I could. In the meantime, my parallel lives in Santa Rita and Santa Fe were engaging and occupied my mind and attention, frequently leading me off in aimless directions, such as...

I'm struck by the incongruity of two articles I stumbled across today dealing with evangelicals and the Christian Right. The first is by Frederick Clarkson, published online. Clarkson sounds an alarm for the threat posed by some evangelical Christians, particularly "the broad theocratic movement we call Dominionism." By his definition, "Dominionism is...the idea that Christians are called by God to exercise dominion over every aspect of society by taking control of political and cultural institutions." He warns that these people and their dogma present a serious threat to the progressive value of religious freedom and must be guarded against at our peril. He points out that the movement has aligned itself with Donald Trump, "whom some evangelicals believe has been chosen by God to help enforce what they call 'biblical decrees.'" Even God has bad days.

The second article appears in the April 2018 issue of *The Atlantic* magazine. The front cover proclaims, "How Evangelicals Lost Their Way: And Got Hooked by Donald Trump." The piece was written by Michael Gerson, a George W. Bush advisor. The thrust of Gerson's piece is that by aligning with a man of Trump's proven moral shortcomings and corrupt behavior, evangelicals have abandoned the last thread in the fabric of their historic progressive religious tradition. For example, Jerry Falwell, Jr. has said that in Donald Trump, evangelicals have "found their dream president."

The two articles leave us with opposing scenarios. One suggests that at least some evangelicals represent an existential threat to religious freedom. The other suggests that evangelicals are on their last legs and seem destined to go down with the Trump ship. As a left-wing humanist, I'm content with the disarray and off-putting extremism of the movement that will probably prove to be self-defeating in the long run.

●●●

In early April, I had two days in Santa Rita with Lynn and had the pleasure of riding back and forth with company, someone with whom enthusiastic conversation and companionable silence were both enjoyable. Lynn was learning about the many little chores that are a part of the cabin rhythm and make it all worthwhile; keeping the fire going, splitting wood and kindling, feeding the birds, clearing the fallen cottonwood in the meadow, and doing the inside routine of cooking, modest housecleaning, and the other minutiae of domestic life.

I had a telephone conversation with Baudelio, and we talked about how dry the meadows looked and agreed it was time to activate the acequias. He had been thinking about getting started on that but was finding it hard to follow his traditional timing. The high water had built up loose logs and debris against the diversion dam gate and needed to be cleared before opening the gate. I suggested that maybe he and I could get together next week to work on that project; something old guys could do together to keep each other out of trouble and dedicate the new season.

Baudelio's older sister, Josie, had moved into the nursing home in La Jara and was happy to be there with better care than her family could provide at home. The north country is full to overflowing with old people, slowly dying despite the loving care of children and grandchildren. They often suffer from the incapacitating ills of the elderly, inadequately treated by scarce and overwhelmed medical caregivers. At least that was my perspective as an old guy talking with other old guys and hearing their stories.

Baudelio reported that a friend's wife had just died after a massive debilitating stroke that she survived at home for five days before succumbing. It's an often-repeated story in the San Luis Valley; old people, many with chronic illnesses, with only limited health care in the richest country in the world, living out their last years in poverty and third-world care conditions. The people here are philosophical and accepting of their fate and don't feel deprived or abused. These are the conditions they have observed and experienced all their lives on the rural, Hispano edge of American life.

Lynn and I enjoyed enchiladas and tacos at the Mesa Vista Café on both legs of our trip north and south. She met my friend Veronica Chacón, my oldest acquaintance among the staff of the Ojo Caliente restaurant. Arriving with a new woman after years of being there with my Chris, and then by myself for a while, did raise an eyebrow. People were intrigued, curious, and pleased that I had a new friend, and she was warmly and enthusiastically welcomed and accepted into the camaraderie of the place.

When I was paying the bill at the counter before leaving, Veronica whispered to me, "I have a secret to tell you. I'm getting a ……………." With my faulty hearing, I couldn't understand what she was "getting" and asked her several times to repeat herself. Finally, I understood that what she was getting was a divorce. Her hushed tone let me know that this was a daunting event in her life, one that entailed risks she couldn't easily measure; what would happen to her house and her employment, for example. I held her hand and told her I was sure it was the best thing for her. She affirmed her decision strongly but said she wasn't sure how it would turn out, because her husband is a brother of the owner of the café and she wasn't sure she "could stay here." (The restaurant? The community?)

I had found my way into the edge of the northern New Mexico Hispano cultural milieu, but the complex fabric of family and friend relationships were beyond my grasp. A breach like Veronica's divorce would surely unsettle connections created over a lifetime. It was clearly not a rash or sudden decision and must have been the product of long, torturous deliberation. She shared the news with me because she was happy about it, confident it was the right thing for her, and she was prepared to deal with the social fallout.

Lynn and I were planning a driving trip to California to visit friends she had been close to while living there. Lynn announced that she wanted to buy a new car for the trip. The old one was quite perfect, a 2010 Subaru Forester with only 39,000 miles. But she was yearning for a new one. "No bells and whistles, and no add-ons," she said. She was firmly committed to "getting the best deal." She had limited new requirements but wanted a remote opener for the hatchback and a rearview camera, and the new car had to be white or at least a very light color.

We went to the Subaru dealership, and as soon as we pulled into the parking area, Josh O'Neil rushed over to meet us. He was twenty-one years old, new at the job, and had funny ear piercings with plastic inserts that made him look like a sociable Martian. He was trying to grow a beard, was enthusiastic, well-spoken, and ready to make his pitch. Lynn was ready too, and armed with Blue Book data, she laid out the ground rules for the negotiation with a skeptical look and a sales resistant tone of voice.

The first dance was over the trade-in value of her car. She recited the Blue Book numbers. Josh didn't look encouraging but pressed on; he said they would look at the car and see what they could do. First, he wanted to tease her appetite with a look at the sparkling new Forester. The on-the-lot inventory was limited in terms of her announced criteria. They first showed us a white one, but it had fabric seats and she wanted leather, and it had lots of stuff she didn't want. They next showed us a pretty blue one that seemed to reduce her commitment to white, and it was loaded with all the bells and whistles, so she tentatively ruled it out. We retreated to the office to get down to brass tacks.

Josh sensed that she kind of liked the blue one, so he started to lay out the numbers. It was listed at $35,000, but they were willing to let it go for $33,650 if they could agree on a trade-in value. He asked what she wanted, and she said $13,000. Josh went away to check with the boss while we cooled our heels, and he came back with $11,000. Lynn rejected that and said, "Why can't you give me Blue Book?" The boss had stepped in and said, "We need to consider putting money into it to make it saleable." (It was eight years old with low mileage, no dents, clean and shiny, perfect, always serviced at the dealership, ready to go out the door.) The boss disappeared and Josh asked again, "What do you need?" She said she needed $13,000. Josh departed for another conference and returned with his boss who was ready with their best offer. He said, "We can make you a special deal if we can close today, and we'll give you the $13,000."

Lynn: "I want to talk to my son." Boss: "Can you talk to him this afternoon?"

Lynn: "No, he's in Montreal. Can we talk tomorrow?" Boss: "No. We're closed on Sunday. Lynn: "I need to think about it." There was clearly a standoff, but there was light at the end of the tunnel. They were desperate to sell, and she was becoming desperate to buy. She had even fallen in love with the bells and whistles. After an out-of-sight conference, the dealer team returned and the top guy sat down, looked Lynn in the eye, and said, "If you give us a refundable deposit of $500, we'll reserve the car until Monday and we'll give you $13,000 on the trade-in." After an agonizing pause, Lynn wrote the check, we shook hands, and departed. Both sides were on tenterhooks. Nobody would sleep well that night, except Lynn, who could sleep through a nuclear attack with her hearing aids out.

On Monday morning, Lynn and I visited the highly respected owner of "Great Little Cars" on Cordova Road. He gave us a thoughtful and convincing analysis of the situation. He said the dealership offer sounded reasonable, and the best cash deal he could offer for her car was $13,500. We thanked him and went straight back to Josh and his hierarchy where we met the number one manager who waited to hear Lynn's decision. Lynn told her she had just been offered $13,500 for her car. The manager grimaced but took the information to her boss and returned a few minutes later to say, "We'll do it. It's a deal."

My role through all this was to be an amazed, impressed, and mostly silent observer. She knew what she wanted. She haggled them to the brink. Lady Lynn is no pushover. She dickered. She hammered out a deal. She's a horse trader. And she was the proud owner of a brand-new Subaru Forester. And it has lots of BELLS AND WHISTLES. And it's BLUE!

We were off on our driving trip to California in the brand-new Subaru and were staying for several nights at The Athenaeum, the grand faculty club and private social club on the campus of the California Institute of Technology, better known as Caltech. It was like stepping back a hundred years. When we arrived on a quiet Sunday evening, there were few guests in evidence, the spacious public rooms were dimly lit, and we were enveloped in the reverent silence of an unoccupied cathedral It was inspired by the original modern Athenaeum established in London in 1824 as a haven for distinguished scientists, literary figures, artists, and, more generally, noble*men* and gentle*men*.

The Caltech version was brought into being by a wealthy philanthropist who made a gift of stocks that was miraculously converted to $500,000 in cash just days before the 1929 stock market crash. The result is a magnificent building and surrounding gardens that carry the regal name, The Athenaeum.

It is still grand and formal, with an aura reminiscent of an earlier day, even as times have changed outside and inside its walls. It carries the breath of formality, elegance, and exclusivity of its early days, when it must have been a de facto white men's club, and much of the ambiance of a London social club persists in its California descendant. Even today, the Athenaeum management reminds members of its dress code for dinner service in the elegant main dining room. The code even charmingly prohibits flip-flops.

Sharing the lovely "Hale Suite" (George Ellery Hale, 1868–1938) with my unmarried partner, Lynn, seemed pleasantly risqué, given the strict regulatory atmosphere, and it was reassuring to see young women and men, probably faculty or graduate students, confidently violating the dining room dress code with impunity. They were even wearing the forbidden denims, and God forbid, flip-flops.

A few days later back in Santa Fe, Lynn and I had drinks and dinner with a couple living at El Castillo. It's a preeminent retirement institution, and coincidently, the benign side of the facility where Chris spent some of her last days. El Castillo is a place where clients are serenely shepherded through their last years. In a corporate sense, the place could be described as vertically integrated. That is, it takes its clients through the progressive stages, from independent living, to assisted living, to memory care, to nursing care, to gentle death. Not a bump in the road. No offense intended. The guests are nice; a gregarious gathering of lively old white folks in the dining room, all seemingly happy with decorous institutional food served cafeteria style, followed by brief conversation and early return to their separate, nearly identical living quarters.

Those in the early stages of their stay have the freedom to disassociate themselves from the more communal activities and carry on their outside lives until their interests change or physical or other limitations require them to rely more on the support systems that allow them to ease comfortably through their last years. Not my cup of tea, but it seems to serve others well.

Lynn's peer group includes people now mostly in their eighties, many of whom came to Santa Fe in retirement and have shared much of their social lives for perhaps a couple of decades, often living at a distance from children and other family. When one travels along with others so close to the same age, it brings home more starkly the impact of aging. My peer group is smaller, partly because of deaths, and my social circle has a more diverse age distribution. I do have "old" friends and have seen other old friends die, but I'm not as constantly made aware of the phenomenon of aging as is Lynn, whose close circle of friends all have such similar "sell by" dates.

These dark thoughts may seem a strange prelude to the brighter, light filled ruminations that follow. Despite our lives having been different in so many ways, Lynn and I find deep common ground and still have not had our first disagreement. Some argue that every good relationship should include its share of arguments, but we flunk that test. We sometimes wonder what we could disagree about, and the only thing we've come up with so far is that she doesn't like okra and I do. And even on that important issue, I contend she'd like okra too if it was cooked right. Despite our age, we are in the springtime of our love and have not really been challenged yet. Maybe we're old enough that we won't have time to find serious disagreements. Besides, at this stage of life, our rough edges have been worn off and we can more easily find the common thread.

But love at our age is not necessarily what our children or grandchildren expect, enlightened as they may be. Sure, there's companionship, shared opinions, likes and dislikes, the pleasure of cooking together, and a litany of other gifts. And then there's physical attraction, passion, even SEX! It's not the same impatient, insatiable passion of the young. It may not always lead to the same cathartic fulfillment, but it is still a powerful connection between a man and a woman, providing great joy and shared intimacy that gives us a profound appreciation of the value of life.

One late summer weekend I made a solo trip north. I did my usual chores and enjoyed a late afternoon beer and conversation with Baudelio. After a light supper, I sat on my porch, feeling submerged in the heart of nature, river, forest, irrigated meadows, a visual and auditory feast. The setting sun highlighted the river and articulated silver streaks across the meadow created by water drawn from the vein of the river into the capillaries of the acequia system that sustained the living tissue of the valley. The waters, untended this evening, follow the lucent paths determined by gravity and the efforts of farmer ancestors over more than a hundred years.

The scene was orchestrated by the bass of the river, the alto of the birds, and the soprano of the tiny frogs who produced stereo pin pricks of sound from hundreds of secret places in the valley. We think of the sun moving toward the western horizon, only occasionally being reminded that it is we who are moving, counting the passage of celestial time in our invented seconds, minutes, and hours. But we are time-driven creatures and insist on measuring our passage through this place using our presumptuous nomenclature.

The birds, the trees, the coyotes I had seen a few minutes before; the deer, elk, bear, and other countless organisms I can't see or don't acknowledge, follow the rhythm dictated by their evolutionary mandate. Some of them make independent decisions in the episodes of their lives, but in the broad scheme of survival and continuity, they follow the rules they were born with.

Our species, or most of us, believe we can control the forces that constrain us, and in the small space within infinite time we occupy, perhaps we can. We can certainly alter the metabolism of the planet where we live. We can change the content of the atmosphere surrounding us and can modify the climate and the weather, and we do change and often disfigure the physical face of our world. But looking out at the natural space before me, the river, the air, the life forms and the sun that has just disappeared, I was encouraged to believe that the forces and epochal powers we do not control will shape the way the future plays out, and that we are just along for the ride.

...

Lynn decided she needed a lockable street-side mailbox that would allow us to be out of town for a few days without worrying about accumulating mail. Responding to her decision, I took the bull by the horns, searched, and found a suitable mailbox. Pressing on to complete the project, I asked for and received a recommendation on a respected handyman from one of the helpful staff at Big Joe's Hardware. I called him and arranged a visit at Lynn's house that produced a handshake agreement for him to do the job.

Jeff was hyper-animated but seemed to be a well credentialed guy with over thirty years of experience doing all sorts of odd jobs; probably overqualified for installing a mailbox, but eager to take it on. He left to sort out the purchase of a metal post, the associated fixtures, and cement that would be used to set the post. I met him at the store the next morning, paid for the goods, and off he went to do the job while I set out on the road north to my cabin for two nights. He had told Lynn and repeated to me that he would charge $45 per hour for his services and $25 per hour for his son who would help. It seemed like a hefty rate, but we were committed, and it was a modest job.

After a stop for lunch in Ojo Caliente, I was headed north, just past Tres Piedras, almost out of cell phone range, when I received a frantic call from Jeff, informing me that the digging had been harder than expected. A culvert at the side of the road risked "losing cement," the project had taken longer than expected, and his bill to Lynn amounted to about $350. He said that Lynn was furious. In fact, he said that "she was really pissed." Jeff was hysterical, and his characterization of Lynn's reaction seemed totally inconsistent with the way I thought she would react.

I said I would call him on Monday and was sure "we could work something out." In his somewhat garbled message, he said he was concerned that Lynn's disappointment with his services would damage his reputation, and he gave me the impression he had not been paid for his work.

As I drove on north, I thought about having two days to figure out how I could reconcile the strong negative feelings (as described by Jeff) for the woman I love, with Jeff's not unreasonable expectation to be compensated at the rate he had proposed at the outset. As I drove on north, I said to myself, "I THINK I can work it out. I HOPE I can work it out. My life hangs in the balance!"

Cancel the amber alert! Call off the cavalry! On my return to Santa Fe, Lynn advised me that the crisis Jeff presented to me in our dramatic phone conversation on Friday was largely a product of his fertile and distorted imagination. She had paid him in full, told him to skip the promised spray painting of the post, and she thought, sent him happily on his way. Jeff didn't call me on Monday. I didn't call Jeff on Monday. Jeff seemed to be a drama queen. Case closed.

The mailbox looked great.

•••

On another trip north, the Mesa Vista delivered again. I was greeted by Cindy with a hug. Veronica came out with a warm smile and told me her pending divorce was going to work out well. That was a big relief. She reported that Jamie Ross was back from Mexico and that he and Tony Chacón had asked for me.

A café visitor, Gilbert Ortiz, introduced himself and told us he was originally from Romeo, up in the San Luis Valley. That's the place that had to remove the "r" from its name because there was already a town in Colorado named Romero. As I finished my lunch, Jamie walked in. As has been his routine for several years, he had spent the past winter in San Miguel de Allende to avoid the cold in Carson where his modest log cabin is dark and uncomfortable in the winter.

Jamie is a wisp of a man, so short and thin that a brisk breeze would blow him over, but he's voluble and engaging. We cherish our conversations. He told me about a stimulating poetry seminar he attended down south. He had traded one of his beautiful prints for the privilege of attending. He had been working feverishly on a poem about a lovely young woman he'd been in love with many decades ago.

She had been a brilliant photographer, studied at the Rhode Island School of Design, suffered from severe depression, and had attempted suicide several times. She finally succeeded by jumping out the window of her twelfth-floor loft apartment on 17th Street in New York City. She had struggled financially with her art during her short life but was honored posthumously for her work. Jamie hopes his poem will match the beauty, ambiguity, and complexity of his subject.

Jamie confided his own history of mental illness during early years in Santa Fe when he suffered from severe anorexia, depression, and debilitating emotional stress that put him on the street for a while. He was rescued by a therapist who found him and managed, miraculously, to have him committed to care in St. Vincent Hospital where he was confined for about six weeks. He was cared for and counseled under the surveillance of the devoted therapist and emerged with a new lease on life, fragile at times, but leading to many years of satisfying work as a painter, a poet, and a friend to countless people whose lives he has enriched. He's still not adequately compensated financially for his art but enjoys an otherwise rich and mostly happy life.

There was more to life than my familiar travel triangle of Santa Fe, Ojo Caliente, and Santa Rita. There was even time to think. My recent visit to Washington had triggered nostalgia for the time, almost fifty year before, when I had a marginal involvement with the process of law making, working with the people, all white men, who held the levers of power at the time. On my daughter Tina's special day, I had been looking out over a shimmering streetscape surrounded by glittering new office and residential buildings. My view was from the brand-new apartment building, Tina's part-time home. It provided an expansive view of the city streets and a park-like pedestrian space patterned with a scattering of symmetrical street vendors' canopies. Across the street was a shiny new office building housing one of the city's prominent law firms. The discreet sign over the entrance read simply "COVINGTON," the name of a long dead founding partner, forgotten by all but a privileged few movers and shakers in this unusual community. From this vantage point, the state of the nation looked prosperous, full of energy and productivity, but in the nearby shadows and the country beyond, things were not going that well for everyone.

Tina had left an hour earlier for the half-hour walk to the Capitol, ready for her inaugural speech, and then on to serve the citizens of her state and the nation to the best of her considerable ability. She was confident, competent, motivated, and certainly one of the most attractive among her ninety-nine Senate colleagues. Like most of her fellow senators on both sides of the aisle, she would do her best to serve the interests of her state and the nation. For all my adult life I had always been on the edge of the political world, sometimes participating, more often observing, and had always believed that the majority of our elected servants try to put the public good ahead of personal, parochial, or political interests most of the time, despite disagreement about what is the common good. Throughout our history, there have been occasional times of crisis or periods of extreme partisan division, when the pendulum has swung in the direction of narrow, tribal, adversarial postures, and this was certainly one of those times. But this would pass, with time, I earnestly hoped. Tina's message that morning would be one of hope and possibility, a testament to the good side of human nature and an endorsement of the capacity of government to enhance the quality of life of its citizens.

In the Albuquerque airport, headed for Washington, I had an unplanned visit with Senator Tom Udall, a good man and a fine senator. His father, Stewart Udall, served as an Arizona congressman and then as secretary of the interior before adopting New Mexico as his home state. Fifty years ago, I met him briefly in Washington and worked closely with his brother, Arizona congressman Mo Udall. I was a young lawyer for the State of New Mexico, part of a New Mexico delegation working with Arizona to seek authorization and appropriations for projects that would allow the two states to use their share of the water of the Colorado River and its tributaries as provided for by the Colorado River Interstate Compact, an endeavor that was controversial and hard-fought.

What I recall from the months and years of hearings, negotiations, contentious committee and floor debates, and votes is that there was a remarkable level of personal goodwill and respect among the competing advocates and legislative adversaries. The arguments were intense and hard-fought, but the disputants seldom impugned the integrity and virtue of their opponents. The familiar phrase is that they disagreed without being disagreeable. It was a display of comity that fed my optimistic, perhaps naïve, belief that government could function with civility.

Her house. My house. They couldn't be more different, but they each have their charm and appeal. Mine is lean, spare, empty of most things from my former life; just a few photos, paintings on the walls, old things that measured out my previous life, and new things to outfit my new smaller space. Gone are thousands of things that evidenced sixty years of my shared life with Chris, and no longer there to trigger memories and remind me of hard disposal decisions. A few artifacts survived the cleanout; old records, folders full of unidentifiable photos, genealogical records and charts that explored the history of the Flints, the Masons, the Harlans, the Idens, the Mitchells, the Yeiters, the Vogels, the Hestons, the Gateses, but they have been winnowed down into files that occupy just one drawer in the library. The result is an efficient, modest space; cozy, comfortable, and easy to care for, but rather on the Spartan side.

Lynn's house provides a more Athenian alternative. It is spacious, warm, and welcoming, and in further contrast, its contents tell more of the story of her life with Tony and even some long-gone ancestors, some of whom handed down treasures, entrusting them to her care. Some of these things have considerable intrinsic value. Most are important because they are loved by her or remind her of those who once owned them. Hers is a house of people who loved books, and the many bookcases are filled with volumes, some ancient, others more contemporary, demonstrating the eclectic interests of those who added them to the collection.

Scanning the shelves, one can almost hear their voices. "Oh, I've always loved that book and remember when it was the talk of the country," or, "That book was signed by the author to Tony. It's a terrible book, but she was a wonderful person." The provenance of other volumes is more obscure. There are dusty old covers with titles suggesting they may have been textbooks, perhaps once belonging to Lynn's great-grandfather when he was at Harvard in the late nineteenth century. Others are beloved novels or books of poetry, treasured many decades ago by long-lost readers. Lynn has made efforts to scale down her collection, but these books have staying power. It's an act of self-amputation to sever them from the library. There are also boxes of aging paper; documents and records, some created, collected, and preserved by generations of family. Lynn has become the archivist of last resort in a large family for whom paper was valued.

For me, hard disposal decisions were inescapable, required by the size of my new house. Except for a few boxes of precious possessions that escaped the guillotine, they are all gone, no longer there to taunt and burden me with separation anxiety. For Lynn and me, being surrounded in her house with the comfort and beauty of things that have been with her for decades is a luxury and a source of pleasure and satisfaction.

We love sharing our very different houses. She admires the efficiency of my little kitchen. I am amazed by her skill in storing dozens of spices in her less spacious cupboard. My little walled patio is cozy for dinner on a warm summer evening. Her spacious porch and patio provide space for a large party and give us a lovely view of the mountains. Her large dining room and living room accommodate grand dinners and entertainments. My tiny combined living and dining room are perfect for intimate gatherings. We take turns sharing our houses and cooking for each other. And we occasionally escape to our separate corners for personal space, private moments, and time to appreciate the greater time we spend together.

The days and weeks pass peacefully, and the few moments of stress and decision making about how to get on with our two houses are soon forgotten. One Sunday in her house with the *New York Times* was comforting and informative. "The Weekly Review" provided a gathering of great minds addressing the issues of the day and helped this passive observer take stock of where we stand on matters of concern. For starters, Kirk Wallace Johnson provided a frightening glimpse at the power of online vigilantes who bullied a respected scientist and forced him to abandon his cherished university post, his home, and ultimately his identity, and beat a fearful retreat from his world.

It was Father's Day and Fred Bruni described the impact of losing one's father, focusing on Barack Obama, David Axelrod, two Obama aids, and Bill Clinton, among others. In Obama's case, Bruni suggested that "grief and struggle foster empathy." These were nice Father's Day thoughts, leaving me with a feeling of warmth and optimism and ready to move on to more challenging matters.

Another book was by an Iraq War veteran who suffered with depression, alcohol abuse, and suicidal tendencies in the wake of "the fiasco that was the war in Iraq." He told us that "books saved my life." In the purgatory of his journey, he stumbled onto a book of poems by Dylan Thomas and found what he describes as "a moment...of grace." It transformed his life.

The *Times* provided other tempting titles, including "Don't Meditate at Work" (I'll think about that), "The Bible's #Me Too Problem" (Surprise!), "The Invisible Black Midwesterner" (Good to be reminded of that), "No, Not All Women Are Democrats" (But we're working on it), and "Psychos on the Potomac" (More good news).

I've always been a fan of the "Book Review," not to find books to buy but for the joy I've experienced, marveling at the passion and sometimes self-absorption of the reviewers. One book was introduced with the intriguing subtitle, "Stripping the Novel Down to its Frame." That almost sounded salacious. I gave the review a try but couldn't find a path through the murky thesis.

The author and the reviewer were totally in sync in the next piece. They were both geneticists. The book considered the current state of knowledge in that field and the startling new discovery that mothers "don't just pass traits to their children—they receive them as well." I couldn't help hoping the same is true for fathers. My children have traits I would like to inherit. What better way to end that Sunday meander than to see the review of Barbara Ehrenreich's critique of the American preoccupation with death. The imposing title and subtitle told it all: *Natural Causes. An Epidemic of Wellness, the Certainty of Dying, and Killing Ourselves to Live Longer*. It was a tour de force, taking issue with "the fantasy that we can cheat the ravages of age and death." The reviewer warned, "Don't take this book too seriously. It could be harmful to your health."

On another lazy, early summer day, the morning papers left a trail of depressing political disasters we compartmentalized and put in short-term storage, freeing our minds for less worrisome fare. Lynn and I were getting increasingly domesticated, and these Sunday mornings were meant to be enjoyed. We laughed about the unintended humor in an article Lynn found in our local paper titled, "Watch Out for Bears in Dry Summer." Bear stories are always fun.

The New Mexico Game and Fish Department's bear and cougar biologist, Rick Winslow, warned of "an increase in conflict activity with bears." The department issued a list of bear precautions and advice for campers and hikers. If we encounter a bear, we are advised to make ourselves "appear larger," presumably to intimidate the bear. It sounds like form of self-aggrandizement, hard to achieve when under stress.

If attacked, we should "fight back using anything at hand and aim for the bear's nose and eyes." Should I try to poke him in the nose with my finger? And we are told that if the bear hasn't seen us, we should "stay calm." Now that's a tall order. Then we're encouraged to "move away slowly, making noise so that the bear knows you are there." If the bear is big and threatening, why would I want to let him know I'm there? There must be something I can remember from *The House at Pooh Corner* that would help me let him know I love bears. But it was the final precaution that really caught our eye and gave us a serious case of the giggles. We were told:

"Give the bear plenty of room to escape and pick up children."

That picture presents a crisis of conscience. If we are hiking with children, should we slowly move away from them, surrendering them to the bear? Will the bear want to adopt the children? What will the bear do if there are no children to pick up?

My partner remembered an example of extreme double entendre from an article in the *Los Angeles Times* many years ago. The writer quoted a witness who reported seeing "a man with a broom in his pajamas chasing a cat." No wonder the cat was running! And the man! How could he run with a broom in his pajamas?

A week later, with time on our hands, I found an unexpected way to plan a weekend getaway. While scanning the bulletin of the Kit Carson Electric Coop, the provider of electricity to our cabin, a little story caught my eye. It reported that the 23rd Annual Weed Bluegrass Festival would be held on July 21 and 22. My first thought was that it might be referring to a musical marijuana fiesta. Reading on, it became clear that Weed was a place and not a product.

I unfolded my New Mexico road map and discovered that Weed is indeed a tiny community in the Sacramento Mountains, twenty-two miles southeast of Cloudcroft. The idea of listening to America's unique folk music in a little out of the way place way down in the southern mountains was too tempting to pass up. Lynn and I made reservations to stay at The Lodge, a graceful old resort hotel in Cloudcroft, and on a promising Saturday morning, we were off on our adventure.

We drove down through Moriarty, Willard, and Corona, bypassing Claunch (one of my favorite New Mexico place names), and on to Carrizozo; not quite a ghost town but with plenty of old buildings inhabited only by ghosts, and one of the few towns with two Zs in its name. We continued south in 100 degree-plus temperatures to La Luz, then east into the mountains to Cloudcroft, where the temperature was a delightful 78 degrees. Time was a-wasting, so we went on down the last twenty-two winding miles to our destination, the tiny village of Weed. The parked pickup trucks and cars told us the bluegrass festival was well underway in what had once been the public school and is now the community center.

If we had been there at nine in the morning, we would have participated in the opening prayer, the presentation of the colors, the Pledge of Allegiance, and the singing of the national anthem. As it was early in the afternoon, we just paid our admission fee and entered the auditorium where we listened to several bluegrass groups with names like The Tucumcari Crossroads, Higher Ground Bluegrass, and Southern Flavor. Those ensembles were mostly pretty good, for pretty local groups, and fun to watch and listen to, but at 2:30, the old school gym rocked to the high caliber picking and singing of "Bobby Giles and the Texas Gales," from over Fort Worth way.

After a brief pause to conduct a drawing for door prizes, we started to phase down our listening time with the more modest offerings of a quartet appropriately called Simple Gifts. The audience of maybe 150 enjoyed the show and meandered regularly between the auditorium and the food concession booths that offered a "wide" variety of high cholesterol goodies. The audience members were all white, mostly old and often burdened with wheelchairs or walkers. Many of the customers showed distinct signs of having previously enjoyed the high caloric potential of food service at affairs like this.

The political leanings of the audience were hard to assess, but when one of the performers mentioned that America seemed to be getting great again, the response suggested there were probably quite a few Trump supporters in the audience. Except for the enthusiastic reaction to the more professional Bobby Giles group, the audience reaction to most of the performances was supportive but somewhat muted and lacking in the joyful intensity usually expected from exuberant bluegrass fans. The crowd seemed to be dispirited, almost melancholy, and the delicate, fragile health of some gave the impression we were observing a concert in an assisted living facility.

We pulled out of Weed in late afternoon, skipping the "band scramble" scheduled for 6:30 and planning to pass up the devotion and gospel music that would be on the agenda for Sunday morning, along with "free rolls and coffee." Our back-road drive to Cloudcroft took us through the high, lush meadows and tall trees of the Lincoln National Forest, and along the charming headwaters of the Rio Peñasco. The dazzling elegance of The Lodge where we spent the night, and the upscale guests with whom we shared a splendid dinner, offered a sharp contrast with the humble ambiance of the old Weed schoolhouse and the unpretentious people gathered there to have their spirits lifted by the old-time music.

The following weekend we were back at our mountain cabin. While there, Lynn and I had a conversation with Chris Garcia. His father, Filemón, died some years ago, but his mother, Aloisa, and many members of the extended family still live in the nearby communities. Chris's great-grandfather, Hipolito Garcia, earned a homestead patent on the steep hillside across the river. We have no idea how long he lived there and how he survived in this harsh environment at the beginning of the twentieth century. Chris's grandparents, however, are a vivid presence in his life, even now, decades after they have disappeared, his memories enhanced by his project to restore their home next door.

Juanita was a tiny woman, standing barely five feet tall, but Chris remembers her as a tower of strength. She was the dominant partner in the marriage, the one who made all the important family decisions and managed the modest sums of cash money that came their way. She raised twelve children and did more than her share of the backbreaking work of managing the house, growing a kitchen garden, harvesting the crops, tending the animals, and doing the countless tasks that keep a household going with no electricity or running water. Her husband, Antonio, was a small but vigorous, sturdy man. He did most of the outside work, often with the help of his growing children, and was the unofficial valley *mayordomo*, the primary caregiver for all the new part-time landowners in the valley.

Chris was baffled by the fact that most members of his extended family, despite being mostly poor Hispano farmers, living hand to mouth in primitive conditions far from centers of power, were almost always Republicans. Surely, times have changed and political parties have changed, but from today's perspective, it seemed strange to him they were so uniformly Republicans, since the policy positions of the Democratic Party seemed more aligned to the needs of his people. It's worth noting that in the late territorial and early statehood years, the Republican Party was dominant in much of the north, including Rio Arriba County. It was only when Franklin Roosevelt and his New Deal appeared on the scene that things gradually began to change. But people are slow to give up their father's religion and party affiliation.

Our conversation jogged Chris's memory, and he recalled snippets that partially explained the political behavior of the old people. His early years were before the advent of big money in politics, but small money did the job quite nicely. He remembers seeing local politicians handing out money or making gifts of food or other necessities to voters to thank them in advance for their loyalty and their vote. And then there were the jobs at the voting places, made available to the "right people." The people in these remote, rural Hispano neighborhoods were just being introduced to the cash economy and politics, and political jobs provided a few dollars, which went a long way to build support, if not to buy votes.

In addition to his ruminations about political habits, Chris also described his frustration with his inability to trace his family line back beyond his paternal grandfather. The old people were often only moderately literate and left little documentary evidence of their lives. Their footprints in the sands of time have long since been erased.

After our visit with Chris, Lynn and I were struck, as we so often are, by the seismic differences between our histories and those of Chris, his family, and neighbors. Prompted by Chris's reminiscences, Lynn began to tell me one of the stories of her family. Her grandfather, Gordon Cilley, lived in Paoli, Pennsylvania, and was the editor of the *Philadelphia Record*. His wife, Maude, was the daughter of Abel Shuford, "a rich carpetbagger" in North Carolina, according to the family story. Maude tragically died when Lynn's mother and her sister were just six and eight. Gordon Cilley found himself unable to manage the care of his daughters without help and decided it would be best to send them off to their maternal grandfather's plantation in North Carolina, where, as was the practice in that postbellum world, they were put in the care of a wonderful, loving mammie named Ann. Ann and her husband, known as Uncle Harry, were a part of the household. Their last name has not survived. Family legend has it that they were the children of slaves who had been owned by the Shuford family. Ann and Uncle Harry were no longer owned by the Shufords, but in a sense, they still belonged to them.

When the girls were returned two years later to their father and his new wife, Marcella Ruth, Ann and Uncle Harry accompanied them and became a part of the Cilley family, relieving the new stepmother of the more intimate and burdensome duties of parenthood. In what was often the southern tradition and practice, transported now to Pennsylvania, Ann, their mammie, assumed a role that was emotionally more like that of the girls' birth mother. It was an intense and loving relationship that continued until the girls reached maturity, when they were ready to move on to college or whatever else might follow. The separation seems to have been absolute, and the fate of Ann and Uncle Harry is shrouded in mystery.

Lynn's mother, Adelaide (Jackie), was off to college, but events intruded to make that a short detour. She had the misfortune to fall madly in love with William Gilbert Ward, a tall, dark, handsome young man of whom her father strongly disapproved. He did what any self-respecting, caring father would do. Enabled by his daughters' recent inheritance from Grandfather Shuford, he sent her off for a year in Europe with a tutor, to round out her education and cool her ardor. The strategy worked as so often it does; she had a grand year abroad that proved the old adage that absence makes the heart grow fonder. She returned home, even more deeply in love, ignored her father's wishes, and married the handsome devil.

Jackie and her sister had become heirs to a substantial fortune that would make their later lives easier. That fortune was slowly spent down over the course of their adult lives. Bill Ward was an incidental beneficiary of that estate. It gave him the luxury of leading a relatively relaxed life, not burdened by the need for steady employment and free to enjoy the good life; golfing, boating, grand picnics, and rowing on the Susquehanna River with John Kelly, father of the lovely and talented Grace Kelly and her brother, John was who was an Olympic rower like his father.

Our conversation with Chris Garcia and the memories it evoked of Lynn's family provided us with an abbreviated tale of two cities; two life paths that could not have been more divergent. But still, both stories, both families, have their share of mysteries and unanswered questions.

...

It was another gift of a day in Santa Rita, without Lynn on this trip. Sometimes a solitary visit is good. Work, when I'm here, is my most treasured play. Today I played at bringing in the firewood. In the local parlance, *Vamos para la leña!* (Let's go for the firewood!)

Just fifteen minutes up the high road through Atencio Canyon is a lovely little aspen grove, shown on page 80, watered by springs that sustain a few acres of these wonderful communal trees we are told are all one organism though appearing to be a stand of many different trees. I'm always happy to be among them, sharing the beauty and peace of the place. It's not always peaceful. There are blizzards and ferocious winds at times, and the weak root systems of the aspen provide frequent deadfalls, giving me the bounty of clean burning, easy splitting firewood.

I found two nice, clean, accessible trees that I could be reached with my truck. I trimmed off the small branches and began to block up the still green trunks. The blocks were heavy with their life blood, but over the approaching winter and next year's spring and summer, they would dry out and be ready for splitting to supply warm fires for next year's fall and winter.

The ceremony of finding, blocking up, and loading the wood is a joy. Fall colors were just appearing, and a few of the thousands of aspen leaves were beginning to make their shimmering golden autumn display. The air was crisp, promising cold nights and frost on the windshield. In the quiet interludes when the whine of the chainsaw was silenced, the stillness was a blanket around me. But there was work to do, and the sweat ran down my face as I brought in the harvest of the most benign of all fossil fuels whose sweet smoke can't possibly be called a pollutant.

The job was done, and I was down the mountain. The new load was added to the impressive pile, and it was time to collapse into a deck chair on the cabin porch for a blessed rest. Later in the day as the sun retreated behind a bank of gray clouds, I was visited by two part-time neighbors arriving on their ATVs from down the road. They were part of a group of four archery hunters, here all the way from Wisconsin and using Baudelio's cabin as their base of operation. They arrived fully camouflaged, their faces painted to make them invisible to the wary elk. I would never recognize them in the supermarket. But the men behind the masks were real people, interesting people with stories and histories I loved to hear. For years they have been coming here for the annual hunt, honoring and respecting their prey and in awe of the habitat it occupies. They have been paying guests of Baudelio, who enjoys their stays.

As the daylight dimmed, we described the outlines of our very different lives, found common ground, shared perspectives, and gained a sense of one another. Jason Meyers was in the last month of a twenty-eight-year tour of duty in the army. He's experienced the Iraq War and assignments in other dangerous places, but he has a clear sensitivity to the commonality he's found with people in Afghanistan during recent time spent there. Jason is a thoughtful and articulate man, educated mostly by his army time and the experience of being exposed to people from other cultures. That life has shaped and polished his perspective and nurtured his respect and sympathy for the real people he has met face to face in the vastly different cultural settings he has visited.

Clay Paulson, a few years older than Jason, also spent time in the army after high school in a small Wisconsin town. He returned to that small town and has worked for the highway department of his home county for twenty years. He is more quiet and reticent in conversation, and his life experience is less exotic than Jason's, but he is obviously a warm, compassionate family man, grateful for the companionship of Jason and the other two members of their group with whom he has enjoyed these years of traveling to this remote place to share time together.

In the growing darkness, we looked at the piece of the natural world spread out before us and enjoyed the pleasure it brought to see this small slice of what nature provides. Though we had been strangers an hour before, we now had a common bond. Our conversation about this space confirmed our love for the beauty of the world and gave me hope. I am grateful for times like this, however delusional they may be. They help me get up the next morning with hope, even joie de vivre, and a cautious belief that things can and will be better. I was glad to have met

Jason Meyers, Clay Paulson, and, later, Andy and Colten Sirek, their partners in this annual adventure.

The hunters' visit signaled the arrival of fall, a lovely season to be enjoyed, to be sure. It's also a time for introspection and acknowledgment of the fragility of the life of all living organisms. As we looked around us, we saw the retreat of life into the season of winter. For some individuals, it would be the end of their existence. For others of us, it would be a recess. Following the rhythm of the seasons and years, the aspen and cottonwoods celebrate with their colorful display. The grasses turn brown. The chipmunks prepare for hibernation. For humankind, the autumn metaphor is compelling. In Santa Rita we thought of Baudelio with a sense of foreboding. His health was in decline. The demands of his occupation were reduced in that season, but his work was never done. The cattle still needed his attention in the fall and winter. Frenchie tried to take on more of his chores, but Baudelio still felt the magnet of responsibility.

Among the part-time residents, some of us would try to visit the valley while the weather made it possible. Most were gone until spring. The previous winter had been distressingly lacking in snow, making it possible to be there even in January. But the new winter was promising, with early snows closing the high road up Atencio Canyon and making the low road through San Miguel problematic. This was the time of year when Baudelio would take a vacation from us as we were out of his orbit for three or four months. We looked forward to that interval with some dread, and we hoped he would rise from the winter shadow in the spring as he had for so many years.

Despite our concerns, life went on in the lower regions of our experience. Instead of worrying about fire danger in the national forest, we agonized over the political firestorms in Washington. One of these arose out of the nomination of Judge Brett Kavanaugh to the Supreme Court. We were distracted from the pleasures and small challenges of our lives and agonized over the credible testimony of his wrongdoing and his strident attacks against his accusers and the senators charged with giving their advice and consent to his nomination. With regret and relief, that episode ended, and we turned back to more mundane challenges.

I often revisit the boundaries between my world and the other worlds encountered in my journey. It's not a physical journey but the random ramble of everyday life that provides chance encounters with people who are in some respects "different" from me. It could be a religious, cultural, linguistic, ethnic, or racial difference, or one defined by national origin or some combination of those factors. People don't fit neatly into categories and can't be arbitrarily pigeonholed. America is a country mostly of immigrants, plus a few remarkably diverse indigenous folks whom we collectively describe as Indians or Native Americans. We are all different in many ways, and despite the passage of time and the erosional influence of long-term proximity, our differences haven't disappeared.

People of my generation were taught the mythic story of a country of immigrants, welcomed to this new land and over time magically amalgamating into a blend of people who would become homogeneous "Americans," evolving into a new species with largely shared characteristics. It was called the melting pot, a metaphor that was demonstrably inaccurate. When I was young, the part of the pot I occupied was filled with a mélange of humanity that had proved to be remarkably resistant to melting. There were Italians, Germans, Poles, Portuguese, Swedes, Norwegians, Jews, and who knew what all. As the years went by, many other hyphenated Americans were added to the list. We met them or heard about them, and the "we" that was "us" often assumed that the new species of Americans would come to be kind of like us.

The presumptive, daring arrogance of that culturally centric characterization of the new Americans is obvious. It derived from a view of our brief history, predicated on the premise that there was an American starter kit comprised of the kind of people who came to these shores on the Mayflower in 1620 or maybe to Jamestown in 1607. It could include some of the other white, mostly Protestant, northern Europeans who came in the next few decades. Over time, as other people arrived, they were expected to miraculously take on the hue and other markers of those who came before.

African slaves were another important contribution to the American blend that made those assumptions even more outlandish. Having celebrated Columbus Day not too long ago, we were reminded that Crístobal Colón, as he's known here in New Mexico, "discovered" America in 1492. We know that while his journey was sponsored by the king of Spain, he was in fact an Italian entrepreneur. And the Anglo oriented view of American history overlooked the settlement of New Mexico by Spain in 1598. Perhaps even more to the point, a source as authoritative as Wikipedia tells us that the place now known as New Mexico welcomed its first immigrants in about 9200 BC, whose descendants we now label Native Americans.

In any event, it's our good fortune we didn't combine into a bland, boring average of all the different human components in our continental DNA, or average down to some presumed superior model. Instead we retained much of our stimulating diversity. If we're lucky and make a little effort, we can encounter fellow Americans who are different from those in our tribe and learn about and enjoy what we can discover from each other and about each other.

New Mexico is a different model of the coming together experience on this continent of people from different heritages. Unlike the eastern invasion, dominated in the early years by the English and other white, mostly Protestant northern Europeans, New Mexico was colonized by Catholic Spanish settlers, many with mestizo blood. The Spanish dominance of the region lasted politically for over two centuries and persisted culturally through the twentieth century, with continuing influence even today. That is especially true in the rural north where Hispanos are a majority of the resident population. The unique northern New Mexico version of the Spanish language is still spoken in many of their homes. In early Territorial days, Anglo men frequently married Hispana women, came to speak Spanish fluently, and were incorporated into the dominant Hispano culture. That included people like Cristobal Carson, who married Maria Josefa Jaramillo, and probably was more fluent in Spanish than in English, and a young lawyer from Rhode Island, Theodore Wheaton, whose mother back east would have been surprised that in the 1850 census, he was listed as *Teodoro*. It was a different kind of melting pot.

I came as an outsider to this Hispano place; first as a lawyer with a young family, living in a majority Hispano neighborhood, with children in an elementary school where most children and many teachers came from families where Spanish was the language of the home. Hispanos were among my fellow workers and new friends. Then I became a landowner along a small northern river with a distinctive Hispano history. Even later, it was our Ojo Caliente restaurant. It was in those places that I had meaningful chance encounters with people who were in some respects different from me. It was my good fortune that I had been prepared for these experiences by studying the language in high school with a teacher who had emigrated from Spain, who taught us the language and introduced us to her country of origin, its people, and the Spanish world.

New Mexico Hispanos have a long history of abuse and mistreatment at the hands of politically and financially advantaged Anglos. It's not surprising that there is still some resentment of that history and residual suspicion of people with that heritage. For trust to be built, for those old boundaries to be breached, risks must be taken by individuals and there must be openness to reciprocity. Fortunately, those conditions exist in Santa Rita and at the Mesa Vista Café, and as a result, we engage together and enjoy learning about our differences and the overwhelming commonality of our lives.

...

Late October provided a blessed event. It was a peculiar day in Santa Fe. It was a fabulous day in New Mexico. It started raining the afternoon of the day before, soaking the soccer players around town and shrouding the city in unfamiliar dark clouds. It wasn't our typical dramatic cloudburst but rather a gentle, persistent, steady rainstorm. It lasted all night and was still with us at breakfast time and even at noon. It was strange and uncommon, a welcome contrast with our frequently destructive wet weather. Perhaps it was part of the new norm as climate change makes its presence known, but this serene storm proved that strange, unusual weather can be benign. Everyone was talking about this slow, soaking blessing that sank into the thirsty soil; not the familiar wild thunderstorms that send a deluge rushing into the *arroyos*, carrying sand and debris toward our intermittent streams and trying to reach our one Rio Grande.

Looking out at this welcome miracle, we gave thanks but reminded ourselves that this outcome was an anomaly, a fluke, and not the norm. The more usual result of climate change for our region is persistent drought, higher temperatures, destructive storms, and devastating forest fires. Despite the gift of this storm, the changes we humans are imposing on our planet are far from benign. The abnormality of this phenomenon provides an occasional benediction for which we say a grateful amen, but in the long run, we will pay a high price for our mistreatment of planet Earth. There's work to do and we should be guided by science, not sorcery.

One morning at the end of November, I attended the funeral Mass for Carl T. (Carlos) Maés, at the majestic Cathedral Basilica in downtown Santa Fe. He was the father of my friend George Maés. The funeral attracted an inspiring gathering of family and friends, totaling by my guess as many as three hundred people. The grandeur and formal ceremony of the ancient Catholic ritual provided a comforting environment for meditation that could be enjoyed even by unbelievers.

His obituary informed us that Carlos Maés, aged 91, was born in Las Vegas, New Mexico, and spent his childhood working on his family's ranch in the community named Maés. It's not a coincidence the home place had the same name as the man since his family founded the little village and gave it their name. The ranch was homesteaded by his grandfather Manuel de Atoche Maés. Carlos served in the army during the Second World War and earned both Paratrooper and Glider Wings.

Attending a Hispano funeral gives one an opportunity to appreciate the strength and resilience of the Hispano culture, well into the twenty-first century. It displays the degree to which Hispanos and Anglos still follow separate paths in contemporary New Mexico life despite the increasing cultural integration of the community. During the hour and a half before the service, listening and watching the celebrants and the audience, it was moving to see that everyone seemed to know one another. Before the service began, people moved freely throughout the grand space, exchanging hugs and kisses. It was a festival of friendship, kinship, love, and togetherness. Looking out at the crowd for familiar faces, it occurred to me that I might be the only Anglo there except, perhaps, for the priest.

After the Mass concluded, the dozens of family members followed the casket to the front of the cathedral, and as he passed, I was recognized by George Maés. Back in my truck a few minutes later, waiting for the departure of the cortege headed to the National Cemetery for his interment with military honors, my phone rang, and it was George. He called just to let me know he appreciated my being there; an unnecessary but moving thank you, attesting to our modest coming together across the still strong cultural and ethnic boundaries.

...

It was a rather nondescript Pearl Harbor Day, December 7, 2018, not a significant anniversary of the event, but it struck me that it had been seventy-seven years since the attack, and I was eleven at the time. Nice numerical coincidence. All of us alive and aware at the time remember vividly where we were when the news arrived. It was a Sunday afternoon, and I recall the family gathering around the radio in the living room. At my age it seemed to be very exciting, and the adults were very disturbed and emotional. Other details escape me, but it was a stunning and memorable event. We often settled by the radio at that time on a Sunday afternoon or early evening, waiting to listen to our favorite programs, but they were canceled on that terrible day. Except for the national disaster, we might have been hearing Edgar Bergen and Charlie McCarthy or Fibber McGee and Molly, or perhaps The Shadow, but not that night.

Soon after, as the draft began to take effect, older brothers of friends were going into uniform and being trained for war. We were all at war and the war was with us all the time. We watched the newsreels between movies, and the radio was on, constantly giving us the news. Gasoline and food rationing affected us all and we began planting our victory gardens. Everyone whose number was called went into the army or the navy, without exception, or so it seemed. There were jokes about medical exemptions (flat feet, bowlegged guys headed for the cavalry), but we all seemed to be in it together. Some people were rich, and some were poor, but it didn't seem to make that much difference, and the differences didn't seem so extreme. There were no "one-percenters."

The war was all around us. We saw men in uniform constantly. Our family lived close to a navy base and we saw Seabees marching by our driveway, even calling a halt sometimes at our lemonade stand, where our parents said we couldn't charge. I can still sing the Seabee anthem. The contrast between then and now is vivid. We are constantly at war, but it has zero effect on our lives. No one from our family or our friends' families is in uniform. We have a seventeen-year-long war that goes on with only rare mention of casualties, deaths, or injuries. There are no apparent sacrifices. Even when the dead and injured are in the news, it seems almost as remote as casualties from hurricanes.

Today's wars are fought by "volunteers," not democratically selected draftees. We view them almost as mercenaries, hired to do the job for us, not real people from our neighborhood, people we know. When they come home, often seriously wounded physically, and more often with traumatic brain injuries, we pause with ritual sympathy, demand that they receive the care they deserve, but their stories quickly disappear from our televisions and from our consciousness.

I'm not comfortable with contemporary Pearl Harbor Days. We're not all in it together today as we were in 1941 and in 1946 when we grieved and celebrated together. Most of the casualties of these wars are "the others" among us. There are millions of our citizens who have suffered or died for the rest of us in these new wars, but they're not celebrated, grieved, or remembered except in the formulaic solemnities of public holidays.

Saturday, December 22, 2018
An email to my Santa Rita neighbors

I regret to inform that Baudelio has suffered what will be a fatal stroke and will probably be in hospice by this afternoon. He is not expected to survive more than a day or two. He is in a coma and not suffering and the family has instructed that extreme measures not be taken to sustain or revive him. I will forward information about funeral arrangements when the end comes and Sandra and Frenchie inform me of the arrangements. We are losing an old friend and seeing the end of an era. Sorry to deliver sad news but glad he's having a quick, painless end. Hope you all have a great holiday.

Tuesday, December 25, 2018
Email to Santa Rita neighbors

Dear Friends and Neighbors,

Our friend Baudelio disappeared over the western horizon at 12:15 on Christmas morning, passing Santa Claus in mid-flight as he was on his way in. His passing was gentle and painless, but his strong heart kept him going longer than the doctors thought possible. Tough old guy, right to the end. Frenchie and Sandra will let me know about funeral arrangements as soon as they are set. I'm told he will be cremated and that he let it be known he wanted to be buried in the little camposanto by his cabin in Santa Rita, so we can all keep track of him. That will happen sometime next year. Frenchie and Sandra have done a beautiful job of caring for him, helping to make his last years good.

The funeral was planned for an early January Saturday. Lynn and I arrived at the Steam Train Hotel in downtown Antonito on Friday afternoon prepared to stay there for the weekend, but it soon became apparent they were not ready for prime time. The room in the old hotel was dreary, and the outside door couldn't be locked. We disembarked and went out to the Antoines' in Mogote. Frenchie and Sandra insisted we stay in Baudelio's house. The house was exactly as it had been when he last walked out or was carried out, full of stuff that will be a challenge for a domestic archaeologist.

The first formal phase of the celebration was the "viewing," from 5:00 to 7:00 that evening at the Assembly of God church in Antonito. It was well attended, the body lying in state, attendees sitting quietly except for some charming children. No words were spoken, just silent meditation and whispered greetings, handshakes, hugs, and hushed conversation. The guests seemed comfortable and familiar with death. Lynn and I had dinner at the Dutch Mill restaurant, followed by a good rest at Baudelio's house and the next morning enjoyed a leisurely breakfast at the same fine restaurant. Then we headed north for the funeral.

It was below zero when we left Antonito, and as we got closer to the low point in the valley, the temperature dropped to minus four. The drive was magical. The sky was clear, and snow-covered mountains were visible in all directions. There was a ground-hugging ice fog across much of the view-scape, and the occasional cottonwoods and willows were glazed with ice, as was every other feature rising above the valley floor. The visual impact was breathtaking. The whole valley was covered with a few inches of snow, a winter wonderland.

It was fourteen miles north to *La Jara* and then nine miles west to *Capulín*, through beautiful farm and ranch country, and finally to the little white *Asemblea de Dios* church, the same denomination as Baudlio's church in Antonito. It was chosen as the venue because it was large enough to accommodate the expected crowd but also because it was so pretty. When we arrived an hour before the service, the parking lot was already crowded, and inside the church, it had the feel of a lively celebration. The gathering was clamorous and exuberant as people greeted each other and visited together. There were people I knew and many more I didn't recognize, most of them Hispano friends and extended family. It was a happy place, full of smiling faces. The Santa Fe crowd included my family and our Kelly partners plus many other Santa Rita neighbors. We saw Chris Garcia and others from the extended Garcia family. I was glad to see Baudelio's friend, Maria Martinez. Frenchie had prepared a photo collage including several pictures taken a few years ago at the cabin. Chris Garcia and seven other Garcia men were dressed more formally as "escorts," honored equivalents of pallbearers, though they didn't handle the casket, which was open through the service and after.

The minister, "Pastor Gil," is a San Luis Valley native and had been recruited by Frenchie, "because he has a good voice." Frenchie describes himself as "not religious" and told me he thinks most preachers "are full of shit," but he wanted Baudelio to be honored in the fashion he would have preferred. Many in Baudelio's family were still traditional Catholics but others, like Baudelio, had slipped away from the faith, perhaps because of the shortage of priests in rural New Mexico and the need of the people for religious connection. Respecting Baudelio's religious affiliation, Pastor Gil is a protestant minister and he was the right person for the role. He was in his seventies, had a grand, sonorous voice, and his sermon, if it could be so described, was almost entirely in Spanish, with occasional partial sentence interruptions in English. His message was free form and his words flowed effortlessly. He had great stage presence, a lovely smile, and a microphone-enhanced, deep, solemn bass instrument he used to great effect. He interrupted his thoughts now and then to sing religious songs in Spanish, accompanied on the piano by an older woman I later learned was his wife. Whenever he paused to gather his thoughts, he uttered a grateful "Alleluia."

Frenchie had informed me I would be asked to do my eulogy in the middle of the program, because the preacher didn't know Baudelio very well and thought my comments would let him become better acquainted. In the middle of a mellifluous Spanish sentence, I heard my name pronounced and rose to take my place at the podium. My remarks were mostly light-hearted, as had been suggested by Frenchie, and touched chords that would be familiar to the audience. It was an honor for an Anglo to be asked to deliver the customary remarks.

When I finished, the minister thanked me and picked up where he left off, continuing his oration for quite a few more minutes. As I returned to my seat in the family section, I was struck by how special it was to sit in an audience of perhaps 200 people, most from families that have been in this country for many generations, and listen to a funeral oration in Spanish that would be fully comprehended by those in attendance. Most of the people were from multi-generational "American" families, often tracing their remote ancestry back to New Mexico and Mexico. Some have moved on to live outside the valley, often with college degrees confirming their mainstream lives. They still retain their old language and cultural identity as Hispanos. The event was touching, and the setting evoked the enchanting diversity of our country and the charm of rural America.

People were reluctant to leave the church after the service. They lined up to greet and hug Sandra and Frenchie and Baudelio's older sister, Josie, one of only two surviving siblings from a family of twelve children. The feeling of warmth and love was tangible, and the bright, cold day added to the sense of gratitude and happiness. The crowd slowly began to depart, and we joined them for the drive back to Conejos and the reception at the parish hall of the Catholic church. Some of the folks seemed to have gone home after the funeral to collect additional family members to enjoy the elaborate catered Mexican feast that was arranged by the family. Frenchie had ordered food for 350 possible guests and there must have been about 300 there, seated at three 50-foot-long tables, often with large extended family groups seated together.

I visited with Chris Garcia's mother, Aloisa, and her family. They reminded me that every September, that branch of the Garcia family comes together for a reunion in the little downstream village of San Miguel. They arrange for a priest to be there to conduct a Mass for them in the little stone church. Sometimes there are as many as 120 family members in attendance, some from California and other distant places. I also had a warm visit with Maria Martinez, Baudelio's friend for the last five years of his life. She asked me to send her a copy of a picture of Baudelio and me that was posted on Frenchie's photo collage.

I've described a mostly happy weekend, but it happened in celebration of a loss. His family, friends, and I will miss Baudelio. By the measure of lives like his, in places like his, with physical, occupational, and health challenges like his, he lived a long life, dying of a stroke at age 76, a way so typical in his rural community. In the more privileged part of the world I inhabit most of the time, we consider death at 76 to be premature. That's not so in Mogote and Antonito. Despite his large family mentioned here, Baudelio leaves only the small remnant of his immediate family; a childless daughter and son-in-law, so his line ends here and that adds to the sense of loss.

For me it was more than that, because, in an unusual way, he had been my best friend. There were other good friends, but he and I had a greater sense of intimacy, perhaps because it required a greater reach for each of us. We came from different life experiences, from different roots, even having different first languages. I've mentioned that he was a quiet man, a private man, characteristics I may share to some degree. We were slow to reveal our inner thoughts and feelings, but occasionally, only occasionally, we broke through that boundary.

I had fun with him. He let me help him with his work. He never really played. He loved to work, and work was his play. He taught me so much about the things he knew that I didn't. He helped me build my cabin. He made Chris laugh and she loved him too. He was fun for my children. Those are some of the reasons I'll miss him. He will be impossible to replace, but I'm grateful I had him as a friend all these years.

...

Baudelio knew everything that happened in the valley, heard all the stories, and was exposed to the eccentricities of all the part-time inhabitants, but he was always courteous, generous, and discreet, never having anything but kind words for the newcomers in his valley and never sharing the stories that could have caused embarrassment. We never heard the disparaging term "gringo" applied to any of us. Chris Garcia had told me that in the privacy of their Hispano conversations we were affectionately referred to as *Los Bolillos* (a name for American whites, borrowed from a kind of breakfast roll!) or *Los Güeros* (a term applied to a blond person).

Baudelio's father, Antonio, had been the unofficial *mayordomo* of the valley, the head man and caregiver for all the mostly incompetent new people. I learned that the real power in that family was his wife, Juanita. By the time we arrived, his father had stepped back and Baudelio was taking over his role as the farmer, rancher, and security provider for the part-timers. He was the man who maintained the five miles of rough road up to Toltec Gorge as well as the road up through Atencio Canyon, making it possible for us to reach this isolated destination.

As the young guy and his father's son, the new folks tended to call him "Junior" or "Baldy" or "Baudy." When I met him and learned his given name, I thought it was a beautiful name and always called him Baudelio. Baudelio and

Arlene taught us the intimate history of the place and their own family story. Santa Rita was given its name by the early settlers who came up the valley in the late 1800s and early 1900s. We don't know if the name was borrowed from an early home of the newcomers of if it was invented for the new one. Those homesteaders were among the last New Mexico pioneers who had followed the little rivers north for centuries to find their new homes.

Without the Garcias, we wouldn't have known the Rio de Los Pinos Valley as a place where people had made a living and where the Garcias still did. It would still have been a beautiful and unique getaway for Anglos with enough money to carve out a camp or rustic resort, but it was Baudelio and Arlene who showed us it was a real place that had been a real community and the *patria chica*, the special place of real people. It was a gift for us to have a working farm and ranch surrounding us, his mother and father's old house on one side and his own cabin on the other.

Baudelio introduced our city kids to horses, and of course, to lots of cows. Tina has memories of a day, many years ago. She calls it the "Hi Ho, Silver Day." Baudelio saddled up a horse for her and the two of them headed up the steep slope through *Cañada Jarosita* toward the Cumbres and Toltec railroad, that takes its guests between Antonito and Chama. They got to the track just as the train came around the bend. The tourists in the open car cheered and clapped, thinking they were seeing a wild west performance provided for their benefit. When the engine was right next to Tina and Baudelio, the whistle blew loudly and Tina's horse shied, whinnied, and reared up on its hind legs. She was scared to death but managed to hold on. When the train was out of sight and the horses had settled down, Baudelio said, "That was a close one." Everyone who knows Baudelio knows he had more than a few close ones. He was a cat with nine lives. Our children and now our grandchildren think Santa Rita is magic and they all have a place in their hearts for the handsome, soft spoken gentleman cowboy who was a special part of their young lives. It wouldn't be right to only say complimentary things about him. There are reports he was sometimes kind of a wild one when he was young. I'm sure occasionally Arlene had to say, "Oh, honey. Don't do that!" I'm sure he scared her sometimes. I know he scared Sandra. I know he scared me sometimes, like watching him steer the fifteen-foot-wide backhoe down the fourteen-and-a-half-foot-wide bank between the acequia and the river.

One of his fascinations was fire. He absolutely loved fire. Sure, it's good to burn last year's grass, dry bushes, and brush to make way for new growth, but it's more than that. It was exciting, fun, and a little dangerous, especially on a dry, windy spring day. Sometimes when we came in on our first spring visit, still a little snow here and there, we'd see evidence of arson. Patches of the fields were scorched and scarred and maybe still smoldering. For Baudelio it wasn't just a springtime thing. One August day we saw him stacking a big pile of debris around an old cottonwood down by the river, right next to the bridge, and we wondered what that was all about. After dark we suddenly noticed a bright shimmering light down that way. When we went out to investigate, we saw that it was a gigantic, roaring fire surrounding the old tree, with flames leaping about a hundred feet into the dark sky—a show that would have put to shame the burning of *Zozobra* at the Santa Fe Fiesta. In the light of that inferno, we saw Baudelio, sitting in his truck in the middle of the bridge, admiring his fire show. When we complimented him the next day, he shrugged it off. It was no big deal, he said. "I just wanted to get rid of all that junk." Oh, sure!

So, that was just for fun. No problem. And he didn't have to use up one of his nine lives. But it didn't always work that way. Frenchie told me about a time he and Baudelio were at an upstream neighbor's place, doing a project involving the backhoe. Frenchie was some distance away but could see Baudelio moving around on the old machine. It had a cracked windshield and two side windows, but of course, the glass was long gone. As Frenchie looked up, he saw Baudelio driving down a side slope at a dangerous angle and the machine slowly tipping. As he watched, it toppled sideways down the slope and out of sight. He ran toward the accident, thinking to himself, "Oh my God. He's dead!" And, "How the hell am I gonna tell Sandra he's dead?" When he came over the rise, he saw the tractor on its side, and there was Baudelio, standing in the middle of the thing, his feet on the ground through one side window and his head sticking up out the other side window, untouched. As he got closer, Frenchie shouted, "Jesus! Are you okay?" Baudelio just looked back at him—and smiled—like a Cheshire cat. There were no casualties and his other tractor was brought in to right the backhoe.

Another time the power went out in the valley as it often did. Baudelio decided the problem was with the condenser down by the Kellys', where the lines go underground. He told Frenchie he had fixed it another time just by poking the condenser with a pole and thought he'd try it again. Frenchie thought he was crazy and said that no way was he going to help, but Baudelio can be very convincing, and he talked Frenchie into lending a hand. Baudelio cut a tall, thin aspen to use as a pole. They backed his truck up to the power pole and put a rubber pad in the bed to stand on. Safety first! Baudelio held the pole, and Frenchie held onto him to keep him steady and reached up to help. They poked. There was a loud crack, and Frenchie felt a sharp jolt in his arm as the current went through his arm into Baudelio, or through Baudelio into his arm. The shock made them drop the pole, and Baudelio was knocked flat on his backside. They were both stunned but not seriously injured. As they recovered, got up, and brushed themselves off, Baudelio said, "I think the last time I didn't use a green pole."

One more close call, maybe one of his last, was in the spring of 2017. He was working on the road just up from the corral where there's a big drop-off down to the river. As he was pushing dirt with the front-end loader, the road collapsed under the left-side wheels, and the loader toppled toward the river. It could easily have flipped several times and ended in the raging stream. Instead, one solid stump was just barely enough to stop it with the machine teetering on its side. It's amazing that the fall didn't toss him out of the tractor and down the cliff into the water. There were no witnesses. Of course, he wasn't even scratched and could never explain how he escaped.

There was another story worth telling, this one not about a narrow escape for Baudelio. It was in October of 2011, and Baudelio and I were taking Jaspar Lopez up through Santa Rita where Jaspar had lived as a child, in the area called *Los Crestones*. The two of them pointed out things they remembered in every nook and cranny along the way, a new story every hundred yards. Every side canyon had a name. Every old cabin or place where there had been one had an old family name.

Coming back down the road, Jaspar excitedly exclaimed, "See that tree? That's where Máximo shot that guy." He said the guy Máximo Quintana had shot was a young man who had met his daughter at the dance hall down in Los Pinos. Jasper recalled that the young man had fallen in love with the girl and started hanging out around her house all the time, unwelcome and making a nuisance of himself. Máximo warned him many times to go away, but he kept coming back, so Máximo shot him, Jaspar said. "Wow. Did he die?" I asked. Jaspar said, "Oh, no. They carried him up to the train, got him to Antonito, and took him to the hospital in Alamosa." There was a pause, and Jaspar added, "And THEN he died." I asked, "Did Máximo get in trouble with the law?" Jaspar responded, "Oh, no. He was a trespasser, and Máximo didn't want him for a son-in-law." Maybe it helped that Máximo was a famous game warden and the closest thing to the law in those parts at the time.

CURTAIN CALL

With his passing and the formal funeral behind us, it seemed unlikely there would be new insights into who Baudelio had been, but I received a letter from his friend, Maria Martinez that gave me a glimpse of a different, more expansive man than the one I thought I knew so well. It described a man who displayed an unselfconscious willingness, even a need, to share trivial and intimate details of his life on a scale I couldn't have imagined.

> *I know Baudelio had a high regard for you. He considered you a good friend. Baudelio and I spoke on the phone a lot (sometimes once or twice a week) for five years. I felt that I had known him longer because we spoke so often. He told me so many stories of his life since his childhood in Santa Rita, his high school years, and his life with Arlene, and of course his trips to and his friends in Santa Rita. Sometimes I would ask him, "Do you realize we have been on the phone for three hours?" Mostly he would talk and I would listen and ask him questions regarding whatever topic he was on. He could talk all night, telling me what he had for breakfast, what he did last week, what he did that day and where he went and who he saw in Santa Rita. He spoke of you often and was grateful you treated him like a good friend.*

Her letter shows what an essential friend Maria was for Baudelio in those last years. It also demonstrates how much more a man will say and reveal of himself in conversation with a woman. It's a gift to learn what Maria added to what I knew about my friend.

On a bitter cold but shiny bright Santa Fe Saturday, early in the next year, the sharp wind had stiffened my fingers on the way to the farmers market. It was always a joyful place, filled with happy shoppers, glad, in that season, to escape the cold and be in the presence of other people and beautiful, tempting products offered by a diverse gathering of farmers, ranchers, and other rural entrepreneurs. I had a pleasant visit with Antonio Manzanares, of Shepherd's Lamb, from Los Ojos and a chat with Matt Oakley, of Berry Beef, from up near Raton. I planned fresh loin lamb chops for dinner that evening, with little potatoes from Matt Romero, from Dixon. With that optimistic frame of mind, it seemed that Baudelio's death wasn't so much an ending as a new beginning. Life goes on, dropping a few people off from one end of the spectrum and replacing them with new ones at the other.

Spring came. It had been a great winter with near record snows, much appreciated after our extended drought. The valley rested under a deep blanket, and the snowpack in the higher country was epic, promising to cling to the mountainsides undiminished until late spring. Our humble river became a thundering torrent as the snow slowly melted with high water likely until late June. I opened the cabin on April 1st, Chris's birthday, and inevitably looked back at my losses, Chris and Baudelio. The days were chilly, the nights below freezing. I saw elk one evening, and as the sunlight slowly disappeared, the stars compensated with enhanced brightness. It was good to be back after four months.

A huge boulder had rolled down onto the upper road during the winter, leaving only a narrow, precarious passage that would be even more challenging with rain. But luck was on our side. A contractor's giant trackhoe had been left up above the obstacle to build a neighbor's bridge, and the machine was used to remove the boulder so that it could exit the valley.

The life cycle of Santa Rita echoes the cycle of all life, resurgent in the spring, retreating in the fall. Baudelio's small herd of cattle, led by an experienced mother cow, found its way over the ridge from Colorado to its summer home, supervised by Frenchie. The people and their animals responded to the solstice and came back by habit to the Rio de Los Pinos. Spring brought a profusion of brilliant, white spears of yucca flowers, and in the early summer the borders of our rough roads would be softened by the delicate, pink blossoms of the wild roses.

It was strange to look across the river and realize that for the first time in over a hundred years, the acequias and fields would not be tended by a farmer. The Memorial Day weekend brought the first significant seasonal residents, all passing Baudelio's cabin with regret that his familiar pickup truck was not there. The overflowing river had created wetlands that produced a fine crop of mosquitos. The cows, sensing Baudelio's absence, found ways to be where they shouldn't be, as they always do. The Fourth of July attracted a good number of family gatherings up the river, some traveling from distant places.

September was the time Sandra and Frenchie chose to inter Baudelio's ashes in Santa Rita. They had commissioned a grand gravestone, so large and heavy that it required the backhoe to lift it over the fence from the road and place it in a little raised garden next to Baudelio's cabin. It is beautifully engraved with a local mountain scene, and under his name and dates, acknowledging his only living descendant, Sandra, it reads:

LAST SANTA RITA COWBOY
WATCHING OVER HER

The early afternoon event coincided perfectly with a nice little thunderstorm and rain. Baudelio would have thought it was hilarious. As people began to arrive, some with raincoats and umbrellas, others completely unprepared, they crowded onto the two little cabin porches while the rain continued. The gathering was a perfect mix of Anglo part-timers, arriving from up above, and the more permanent Hispano relatives and neighbors from the lower valley. The weather and the narrow porches crowded the diverse crowd together, reviving old friendships and stimulating new ones. We all chatted, laughed, and told stories in ways that wouldn't have happened without the weather.

Just in time, the rain stopped, and the brilliant New Mexico sunshine and warmth returned. Frenchie called us to the marker, brought out the urn, placed it by the small hole in the ground next to the stone, and gave a grand, informal talk about Baudelio and his deep love for the place. There were additional remarks from a few friends and family, some choking up with emotion. Baudelio's older sister, Josie, one of only two survivors of the twelve Garcia children, was there and given hugs and kisses by all. She said it was the first time in thirty-five years she had been to Santa Rita. Frenchie placed the urn in the shallow grave and invited several men from the family to place ceremonial shovels of dirt. Flowers were placed on top, along with two cans of Miller Lite that had been provided by a thoughtful guest, in memory of Baudelio's two-can limit in his later years. It was a perfect, glorious event, one Baudelio would have applauded, both for its warm emotional content and its lack of formality.

It had been a fitting end to the summer and to an era, or perhaps, two eras. Baudelio was the last survivor of the band of people who had created Santa Rita. And, with his death, the era of Anglo newcomers sharing Santa Rita with the Garcia family also ended. Granted, Sandra and Frenchie are still with us, but the last real Santa Rita cowboy is gone.

There are other stories and memories that could be recalled, but I'm reminded of the last time I saw him. It was only a few weeks before he died. I didn't know he was in the valley that day. He was always working at something, and this time, like thousands of other times in his life, it was the acequia. I looked out my window and saw a man across the river, above the meadow, slowly walking along the acequia bank with his shovel on his shoulder. I had seen him like that hundreds of times and will remember him that way.

Our memories either compress or expand our perception of the passage of time. Time is not best measured by clocks and calendars. It is best measured subjectively. We often say, "It seems like only yesterday..." Or sometimes, "It's been ages since..." In my case, it's been ages since I began this journey. But it seems like only yesterday that Chris was here, Lynn became part of my life, and I first saw Baudelio walking down the ditch bank with a shovel over his shoulder.

REFERENCES

Adichie, Chimamanda Ngozi. *Americanah*. New York: Anchor Books, 2014.

Allende, Isabel. *The Sum of Our Days*. New York: Harper Perennial, 2009.

Bacon, Francis. *Bacon's Essays and Wisdom of the Ancients*. London: William Pickering, 1852.

Bainbridge, David, Athena Swentzell Steen, and Bill Steen. *The Straw Bale House*. White River Junction, VT: Chelsea Green Publishing Company, 1994.

Bakewell, Sarah. *How to Live: Or a Life of Montaigne*. New York: Other Press, 2010.

Clarkson, Frederick. "Religious Freedom Is a Progressive Value." *ALTERNET*, February 16, 2017. https://www.alternet.org/2017/02/religious-freedom-progressive-value/.

Gerson, Michael. "How Evangelicals Lost Their Way and Got Hooked by Donald Trump." *The Atlantic*, April 2018.

Nostrand, Richard L. *The Hispano Homeland*. Norman, OK: University of Oklahoma Press, 1992.

Proust, Marcel. *Swann's Way*. New York: Random House, 1981.

Chavéz, Fray Angélico. *My Penitente Land*. Santa Fe, NM: Museum of New Mexico Press, 1993.

.

CPSIA information can be obtained
at www.ICGtesting.com
Printed in the USA
LVHW071456300821
696471LV00016B/2509